TOLERANCE

TOLERANCE
Towards an Ethic of Solidarity and Peace

BERNARD HÄRING - VALENTINO SALVOLDI

TRANSLATED FROM THE ITALIAN BY EDMUND C. LANE, SSP

ALBA·HOUSE   NEW·YORK

SOCIETY OF ST. PAUL, 2187 VICTORY BLVD , STATEN ISLAND, NEW YORK 10314

Originally published in Italian by Edizioni Paoline fsp under the title
Tolleranza: per un'etica di solidarietà e di pace.

Library of Congress Cataloging-in-Publication Data

Häring, Bernhard, 1912-
  [Tolleranza. English]
  Tolerance: towards an ethic of solidarity and peace / Bernhard
Häring, Valentino Salvoldi : translated from the Italian by Edmund C.
Lane.
    p. cm.
  Includes bibliographical references.
  ISBN 0-8189-0738-X
  1. Toleration. 2. Christian ethics — Catholic authors.
I. Salvoldi, Valentino. II. Title.
  BJ1434.H3713   1995
  179'.9 — dc20   95-13193
                                                  CIP

Produced and designed in the United States of America by the
Fathers and Brothers of the Society of St. Paul,
2187 Victory Boulevard, Staten Island, New York 10314,
as part of their communications apostolate.

ISBN: 0-8189-0738-X

Printing Information:

Current Printing - first digit   1   2   3   4   5   6   7   8   9   10

Year of Current Printing - first year shown

1995   1996   1997   1998   1999   2000

Acknowledgments

The authors wish to express their thanks to Paola Negroni and Roberto Moretti for their suggestions regarding the development of the first three chapters, those friends who gave a critical reading to the text, Renata Carissoni, Luciana Bonomi, Maria Letizia and Massimo Trisolini and also to Sister Olimpia Cavallo for having conceived this project.

Table of Contents

Introduction

"Necessary" and at the same time "not legislatable," tolerance seems destined in our day and age for an inescapable rendezvous with history.

Notwithstanding all the laws restricting immigration, the population responsible for the phenomenon known as the demographic explosion will continue to migrate, even to the point of replacing the majority in the places to which they move. This is an irreversible phenomenon: one cannot hold back the tides of history.

This situation ought to make us intelligently tolerant so as to permit a gradual, painless passage toward this new multiracial society. In fact, however, we are witnessing a preoccupying increase in episodes of intolerance and a rekindling of nationalistic, ethnic, cultural and religious claims. For these reasons, the United Nations has felt the need to make 1995 the "International Year of Tolerance," seeing this as a condition and foundation for peace on earth.

As always, coexistence, among peoples and nations, comes about and is driven by two different forces: on the one hand the search, the affirmation and the defense of one's own identity; and on the other hand the aspiration for exchange and encounter, with the consequent acceptance of change. The transformation (of oneself, of the group to which one belongs, of the culture of one's own people), that is brought about in the mix or in the encounter with others who have different lifestyles and cultures, is seen by some as an enrichment and a fulfillment, by others as a danger and a pollution. Especially problematic, and at times painfully so, is the presence of this dualism in the religious field, where the conviction of believers that they belong to the one true religion must exist side by side with a manifestation of respect, acceptance, and even love for those who differ.

The scope of this reflection on tolerance is first of all to contribute to harmony in the world, showing how, in living together, the search for exchanges, encounters and common values must prevail. The challenge that this offers is that of knowing how to defend and maintain our own identity (as persons and as a people) in the context of all the values that we hold to be universal and, at the same time, to open ourselves to comparison and negotiation especially when it comes to defining that which is of value.

Another scope of this reflection on tolerance is to contribute to an increase in the conviction that tolerance is a universal value, fundamental to building peace and solidarity.

In this book various meanings of tolerance and the diverse situations in which it can be manifested and put into practice will be examined, but above all the psychological, anthropological and ethical foundations for tolerance will be sought and pointed out. Tolerance is being imposed upon us today by the need for survival itself. Nevertheless it will be proposed in this book as a "conscious choice" with the intention of living it as the highest form of love, and — even more — of the love which is anchored in the Christian message where the command to accept others is so impelling as to include even enemies in one's love.

Tolerance, solidarity, and fraternity are three moments in the one path to God and to the full realization of oneself as a human being.

The first stage in this journey is tolerance understood and lived not as a passive endurance of conflict, but as a joyous daily struggle, an active search for the proper point of encounter between ourselves and those who are different. More than ever our world today needs tolerance in order to preserve the existence of humankind on earth; yet the very instinct to self-preservation brings us to perform acts of intolerance.

To understand this paradox is of fundamental importance

because, beyond theoretical disquisitions, life on our planet depends precisely on our capacity to coexist with others, respecting them and their diversity. The destructive potential present on earth in fact is already incredibly elevated and we can not permit ourselves an escalation of armed conflict which could bring about our own self-destruction. This is one of the motives which requires us to study exhaustively the theme of tolerance. To know a reality in depth is the first step in understanding and changing, in orienting ourselves and choosing knowledgeably, without allowing events to establish the rules of the game.

But what do we mean by the terms "tolerance" and "intolerance"?

The American Heritage Dictionary defines tolerance as

(a) the capacity to endure hardship or pain (from the Latin *tolerantia*, derived from *tolerare*, to bear);
(b) the capacity for or the practice of recognizing and respecting the opinions, practices or behavior of others.

Two aspects of this term are immediately clear: etymologically, in fact, the meaning of "to tolerate" is "to endure," with a clear passive connotation, while this aspect is no longer perceivable when we intend the term in its second sense. In this second sense "tolerance" takes on a positive value, linked to a particular way of managing conflicts.

Schematically, one can underline three ways of handling conflict, each associated with a different kind of conduct. In the case of a conflict resulting in attack, we cannot talk of tolerance; in the case of retreat, we are closer to tolerance in its passive significance of enduring; only in the third case, where there is negotiation, can we speak of coming face to face with tolerant behavior in the full and positive sense of the word.

Possible modes of dealing with conflict:

a. attack (aggressive behavior);
b. retreat (passive behavior);

c. negotiation (assertive behavior — the affirmation of a
   value).

It is in this special sense of "negotiation" that we intend
"tolerance": as a value to be pursued, as a way of acting led by a
reasonable and realistic analysis of oneself and the other (the subject
of the relationship), and as a path to solidarity.

Biblical Abbreviations

OLD TESTAMENT

Genesis	Gn	Nehemiah	Ne	Baruch	Ba
Exodus	Ex	Tobit	Tb	Ezekiel	Ezk
Leviticus	Lv	Judith	Jdt	Daniel	Dn
Numbers	Nb	Esther	Est	Hosea	Ho
Deuteronomy	Dt	1 Maccabees	1 M	Joel	Jl
Joshua	Jos	2 Maccabees	2 M	Amos	Am
Judges	Jg	Job	Jb	Obadiah	Ob
Ruth	Rt	Psalms	Ps	Jonah	Jon
1 Samuel	1 S	Proverbs	Pr	Micah	Mi
2 Samuel	2 S	Ecclesiastes	Ec	Nahum	Na
1 Kings	1 K	Song of Songs	Sg	Habakkuk	Hab
2 Kings	2 K	Wisdom	Ws	Zephaniah	Zp
1 Chronicles	1 Ch	Sirach	Si	Haggai	Hg
2 Chronicles	2 Ch	Isaiah	Is	Malachi	Ml
Ezra	Ezr	Jeremiah	Jr	Zechariah	Zc
		Lamentations	Lm		

NEW TESTAMENT

Matthew	Mt	Ephesians	Eph	Hebrews	Heb
Mark	Mk	Philippians	Ph	James	Jm
Luke	Lk	Colossians	Col	1 Peter	1 P
John	Jn	1 Thessalonians	1 Th	2 Peter	2 P
Acts	Ac	2 Thessalonians	2 Th	1 John	1 Jn
Romans	Rm	1 Timothy	1 Tm	2 John	2 Jn
1 Corinthians	1 Cor	2 Timothy	2 Tm	3 John	3 Jn
2 Corinthians	2 Cor	Titus	Tt	Jude	Jude
Galatians	Gal	Philemon	Phm	Revelation	Rv

TOLERANCE

— I —

Rigidity, Impatience and Altercations: Manifestations of Intolerance

THE FACES OF INTOLERANCE

The history of humankind is characterized by a long succession of conflicts. It's important to recall that from ancient times human beings have struggled to live peacefully side by side, having recourse for the most part to exclusion or marginalization to keep under control whole social groups or "castes," defined on the basis of their economic activity, their wealth, their ancestry, or their race.[1]

Moreover, it must be stressed that religion has frequently contributed to making such conflicts "holy," thus justifying divisions.[2]

It is not simply a matter, however, of past history. Our newspapers present us with episodes of intolerance every day, whether lived within the confines of the walls of one's own home or on the battlefield, e.g. in Rwanda or the former Yugoslavia.

Our own vocabulary can often be a significant and revealing

---

[1] A few examples will suffice to situate us in the historical context: the persecutions of Christians in imperial Rome took place prior to the Edict of Constantine (313 A.D.); the invasions of foreigners and their stigmatization as "barbarians" on the part of Christians in the High Middle Ages; the religious wars: against Islam, heretics, within the Christian world between different confessions, against all atheistic thought, lay or scientific; the extermination of entire populations tied to the conquest of new lands and new continents; the segregation and persecution of whole peoples and/or races considered inferior, dangerous, demoniacal, etc.

[2] Such is the case, for example, of the Indian "caste" system, explained by means of the generation of diverse social groups in reference to the different parts of the body of the god Brahma.

1

sector of inquiry into the thoughts and prejudices which roost in our minds. In fact, words like foreigner, different, barbarian, vandal, Jew. . . have assumed very clear negative connotations.

The conviction of the equality of all human beings is only a recent achievement of the Western world. In the democratic Athens of Pericles[3], women, foreigners and slaves were excluded from those who were citizens. The Middle Ages were characterized by the affirmation of feudal power based on blood ties and only with the birth of the commune was a broader political participation permitted. The Modern Age, symbolically inaugurated with the "discovery" (perhaps more correctly, the "conquest") of the American continent, was characterized by the greatest manifestations of intolerance seen up to that time (the extermination of the Indians, the Spanish Inquisition, witch hunts, etc.). And it took precisely this situation to arouse, in Enlightenment thought, the birth of a reflection on the equality of all human beings and on tolerance.

According to Voltaire (1694-1778), religion certainly was not innocent in this area, for persecutions, tortures, trials, "auto da fe's,"[4]

---

[3] Pericles led the city of Athens from 461 to 429 B.C. In this period the city reached the apex of its economic and military power and at the same time the pinnacle of its cultural development.

[4] "Auto da fe" means literally (from the Portuguese) "act of faith." From 1481 it was, in Spain and in its colonies, the solemn sentence proclaimed by the tribunal of the Inquisition against an offender; the same name later indicated the condemnation of a heretic to the stake. For this grave error and others, Pope John Paul II proposed in the Consistory of May 1994, that the Church begin its celebrations of the year 2000 by publicly seeking pardon. He expressed this beautifully in his recent apostolic letter, *Tertio Millennio adveniente*:

35. Another painful chapter of history to which the sons and daughters of the Church must return with a spirit of repentance is that of the acquiescence given, especially in certain centuries, to intolerance and even to the use of violence in the service of truth.

It is true that an accurate historical judgment cannot prescind from careful study of the cultural conditioning of the times. . . Yet the consideration of mitigating factors does not exonerate the Church from the obligation to express profound regret for the weaknesses of so many of her sons and daughters who sullied her face, preventing her from fully mirroring the image of her crucified Lord, the supreme witness of patient love and of humble meekness. From these painful moments of the past a lesson can be drawn for the future, leading all Christians to adhere fully to the sublime principle stated by the Council: "The truth cannot impose itself except by virtue of its own truth, as it wins over the mind with both gentleness and power."

holy wars and civil wars are the products of the plague of intolerance towards those of a different faith. In his *Philosophical Dictionary*, under the word "tolerance" we read: "What is tolerance? It is the natural adjunct of humanity. We are all full of weakness and error; we reciprocally forgive one another our stupidity; it is the first law of nature. . ." The final prayer in his *Tract on Tolerance* is especially meaningful:

> It is not, therefore, to men but to you, God of all beings, of all the world, of all times, that I address myself: if it is licit for weak creatures, lost in immensity and imperceptible from the rest of the universe, to dare ask something of you, who have given all, of you, whose decrees are immutable and eternal, deign to look with mercy on the errors which flow from our nature. Grant that these faults don't result in our misadventure. You who did not give us a heart with which to hate one another, nor hands to cut each other's throats, grant that we help one another to support the burdens of this difficult and fleeting life. Grant that the little differences between the clothes which cover our weak frames, between all our inadequate languages, our ridiculous customs, our imperfect laws, our callous opinions, our convictions so unequal in our own eyes yet so equal in your own, in sum, that all these little shadings that distinguish the atoms called "men" don't be-

---

The cardinals in the Consistory suggested that the Church look more to the errors of the present than to the faults of the past. Pope John Paul also addressed their concerns in *Tertio Millennio adveniente*:

36. Many Cardinals and Bishops expressed the desire for a serious examination of conscience above all on the part of the Church of today. On the threshold of the new Millennium Christians need to place themselves humbly before the Lord and examine themselves on the responsibility which they too have for the evils of today. The present age in fact, together with much light, also presents not a few shadows. . . [W]ith respect to the Church of our time, how can we not lament the lack of discernment, which at times became even acquiescence, shown by many Christians concerning the violation of fundamental human rights by totalitarian regimes? And should we not also regret, among the shadows of our own day, the responsibility shared by so many Christians for grave forms of injustice and exclusion? It must be asked how many Christians really know and put into practice the principles of the Church's social doctrine.

come other signals for hate and persecution. See to it that those who light candles in midday to celebrate you support those who are content with the light of your sun; that those who cover their habits with a white mantle to say that it is necessary to love, don't detest those who say the same thing wearing a cloak of black wool; that it be the same to adore you with a chant that is born of a language that is dead or of one that is more recent.

Grant that those whose clothing is dyed red or violet, who require a little part of a little pile of this world's mud, and who possess some round fragment of a certain metal, enjoy it without being proud of that which others call "lavishness" and "riches," and that the rest look upon them without envy: because you know that in these vain things there is nothing to envy, nothing to take pride in.

May all men remember that they are brothers! May they hold in horror any tyranny exercised over the soul, as they hate the brigand who forcefully robs them of the fruit of their labor and their peaceful undertakings! If the scourge of war is inevitable, let us not hate, let us not tear each other to pieces in periods of peace, and let us fill the brief instant of our existence by blessing together in a thousand different languages, from Siam to California, your goodness which you bestow on us in this instant.

The basis for tolerance is to be found in the fact that all men are equal by nature, they have the same weaknesses and the same aspirations to happiness.[5]

---

[5] The concept of tolerance to which we are referring is based on that positive attitude as opposed to others which draw from nonviolence the strength to endure evil rather than to inflict it on others. We are a long way from the spirit which brought the Austrian Emperor Joseph II to promulgate his "Edict of Tolerance" in 1781, and from the attitude of those who "tolerate" others, feeling within themselves however a sort of disdain for them. His was an edict typical of the times; it perfectly reflected a mentality which was very much alive up to the Second Vatican Council: in Catholic countries, citizens of other religions were perhaps tolerated, but not judged equal to the so-called "practicing" Catholics.

The French Revolution (1789-1799) demonstrated the problems associated with translating into practice an ideal ("liberty, equality, fraternity" was the slogan behind the revolution) and the tremendous consequences of the distortion of Enlightenment principles. Notwithstanding the bad historical copies of the original idea, the contribution of the Western world to the community of humankind has at its core the concept of liberty and equality born of the Enlightenment philosophy and expressed in even more rudimental forms in the Declaration of Independence in 1776 on the part of the American colonies and in the first Declaration of the Rights of Man and of the Citizen in 1789 on the part of the French Constituent Assembly.[6]

---

[6] From the Declaration of Independence of the United States of America (1776):

> We hold these truths to be self-evident: that all men are created equal; that the Creator has endowed them with certain inalienable rights; that among these are life, liberty and the pursuit of happiness.

From the Declaration of the Rights of Man and of the Citizen (1789):

> 1. Men are born and live free and equal in their rights. Social distinctions cannot be founded on anything other than the common good.

> 4. Liberty consists in being able to do all that does no harm to others. Thus the exercise of the natural rights of each individual has no limits other than those which assure to other members of society the enjoyment of these same rights. These limits cannot be determined by law.

> 10. No one is to be disturbed because of his opinions, even religious ones, so long as these do not upset the public order established by law.

> 11. The free communication of thoughts and opinions is one of the most precious rights of man. Every citizen can, therefore, speak, write and publish freely, on his own responsibility for abuses of this freedom in cases determined by law.

It's interesting to note how in some passages of the second document (e.g., the reference to not disturbing public order) it is possible to detect the hidden seed of a new intolerance which will manifest itself in the course of succeeding revolutionary phases. Intellectual advancement for that reason struggles to become practical advancement, and this not only at the time of the French Revolution but also today; after two centuries of reflection on the principles of equality among human beings, the examples of nationalist politics, of ethnocentric and intolerant behavior are a daily reality, and not only in the press or on TV.

SPHERES OF INTOLERANCE

The path to tolerance is not only a laborious historical process, it is a daily challenge that involves us entirely, touching all the different spheres of our social life.

a) The Personal Sphere

It may seem paradoxical, but it is necessary to know that one can be intolerant even towards himself. Such is the person who does not accept himself fully, who disapproves of himself or judges some aspect of his own character negatively: such is, in conclusion, the human being who does not know how to forgive himself nor how to pick himself up and begin all over again. It is useless to point out the bag of woes and suffering that can accompany a person who lives in such a condition. An individual must know how to reconcile himself with his darker side. The person who cannot accept his own darker side, will never be able to accept the darker side of others. Even depth psychology requires that a person, for his own good, be reconciled with himself and accept his own limits. Only then can his dark side be transformed into light.

If we do not pardon ourselves, we will not be able to pardon others either and we will waste our time looking for excuses and absurd justifications for our own and others' failings.

Only he is free who accepts his own mistakes and does not make of his error a tragedy, but puts his confidence in the forgiveness of God who throws a feast in heaven every time a human being lifts his eyes to him, more content in pardoning than we are in sinning.

b) The Micro-Social Sphere

By the micro-social sphere we mean the whole network of interpersonal relations which we weave around us and which take in a restricted number of other individuals with whom we have a significant relationship. Even at this level, in the family, at work, in one's peer group, intolerant behavior is often manifested. It doesn't take much to shut others out: to know someone requires effort and so to remain superficial, on the level of appearances, on the outside, is easier. And so we arrive at misunderstanding and even intolerance. If we don't listen, if we don't put ourselves in the shoes of the other, it will be very hard for us to understand his behavior and still more difficult yet to "tolerate" (in this case "put up with") it.

Many, many examples can be cited from an analysis of our own family life: not everything that is new is wrong, nor should all that is old be considered antiquated. Between couples, parents, children, brothers and sisters, there often arises differences and contrasts. To overcome them, one can choose the way of intolerance which is based on inflexibility and presumption, or that of love which is based on acceptance and respect.[7]

Again on the micro-social level, a clear example of intolerance as an incapacity to accept another's point of view is verifiable in some football fans who use the Sunday game as a kind of ritual to vent the aggressivity of the group.

An example of intolerance that is less eclectic but no less sinister is apparent in the social behavior of some associations which are strongly aligned ideologically. The key element for the birth of intolerant behavior is that ideological membership which often carries with it a refusal to dialog, and at times even to have any contact with other similar organizations; these become perceived as "enemies" or "competitors," because they represent differing ideological points of view.[8]

c) The Macro-Social Sphere

It is within the ambit of relationships between large social groups that the most inhumane and cruel consequences of intolerant

---

[7] It's good to recall however that to accept another does not exclude walking, reflecting, and correcting eventual mistakes together.

[8] For ideology we intend here a system of ideas and principles behind a political or religious movement, and so forth, which considers itself — or is lived — as irrefutable, absolute.

attitudes are manifested. According to the case, we can speak of ideological rejection, nationalism, integralism, or racism, but all of these forms of intolerance bring with them situations of rejection, marginalization, exclusion or the negation of others.

Ideological confrontation, in democratic regimes, is a less cruel form of intolerance and it is easily checked in the political life of every country through the dynamic of opposing political parties, where often ideological "rejection" is replaced by democratic debate: that which counts is not so much the common good as the affirmation of one's own position, of one's identity with a party. In this case, one can reach a rigid partisanship, with a dynamic based on opposition and not on real criticism. The content set forth in the program of a political group can lose significance and become an ideological instrument of contrast with a consequent reduction in the possibility of dialog.

With the term "nationalism" we intend that ideology which exalts the value of belonging to one nation or to one state.[9] It is a relatively recent historical phenomenon,[10] induced, not spontaneously, because most modern states have been built by unifying, in the same territory and under the same power structure, people of diverse languages and traditions. The nationalistic idea was responsible for creating a pedagogy based on love of country, the rereading of history from this point of view, and on the official approval of the culture and language.

The nationalistic ideology has been made use of to foster aggression, but in reality nationalism seems incapable of creating a positive union because it is founded on a limited and distorted vision

---

[9] By the term "state" we mean that territory inhabited by a people under a single government; the term "nation" instead does not necessarily contemplate a territorial element, but refers more to a people with a common language and culture.

[10] We can speak of the "romantic" origins of nationalism, precisely because it was in the first half of the nineteenth century that the myth of country and nation came into full flower in response to the imperialism of Napoleon. History shows in fact long centuries of rule and empires which were both multiethnic and multilingual: the first "nation states" go back to the fifteenth century, but only later was the ideology of the state affirmed.

of the sense of belonging, understood as separation from the outside and a covering over of internal differences. A clear example of suppressed nationalism was given by the recent explosive encounters in Eastern Europe with the collapse of Communism; once the external enemy was gone, internal partisanship was exalted with terrible results at times, as for example in the former Yugoslavia.

When the identity of a group is based on religious elements, a form of intolerance known by the name of "integralism" can be born. Nor is this a characteristic limited to the Islamic world as one might deduce from recent facts in the news, but its possible development is inherent in all religions if these hold their members to be a chosen people and who therefore exclude others and denigrate those who profess a different creed. History has demonstrated countless examples of religious integralism within the Christian world, Catholic and Protestant, in the Muslim world and in other institutionalized or natural religions. Even in these cases, the dynamics which favor the birth of integralism are strictly tied to the sense of group identity which holds itself to be the sole possessor of divine truth and which considers the other, for that reason, not only an enemy but even, in the dynamic of religious categories, an instrument of the Devil and for that reason even more dangerous. It is under this banner of accusation that heretics and witches were put to the stake, that holy wars were fought and continue to be fought, that acts of fanaticism and religious terrorism are manifested.

At the pinnacle of the pyramid of intolerance we can locate "racism" with all its manifestations of rejection and eradication in a confrontation with those who belong to a different race. Granted that the concept of race within the human family has scarce scientific validity, the common acceptance of a racial distinction has generated a hierarchy of advantages for some human groups at the expense of others. Even in this case, the need to belong, typical of every individual, finds a response in an identity that is rigidly protected, in a "we" limited and afraid of others which defends itself with the arms of denigration, exclusion, and aggressivity.

MANIFESTATIONS OF INTOLERANCE:
A CONCEPTUAL OUTLINE

1. On the Individual Level:	Rigidity
2. On the Micro-Social Level:	Impatience
	Exclusion
	Contempt
3. On the Macro-Social Level:	Ideological Clashes
	Nationalism
	Integralism
	Racism

— II —

The Roots of Intolerance

PREMISE FOR AN "ANTHROPOLOGY OF INTOLERANCE"

Why is it so difficult to be tolerant, even when its value is understood? Why, using the words of the apostle Paul, is there in us the desire to do good, but not the ability to do it (Rm 7:18)? To respond to these questions, it seems important to us to go to the roots of intolerance, to try to analyze some of its biological and psychological components which have a particular profile in human life and the knowledge of which can prove useful. Understanding, for its part, constitutes in fact the condition for the exchange of opinions, and then from some attitudes and ways of conducting ourselves a useful instrument may come to light which will help us to arrive at a more tolerant way of acting.

So as not to distort the significance and the value of the reflections which follow, certain premises are necessary:

a) Given the complexity of the theme and the multiplicity of points of view, we will limit ourselves to underlining a few specific questions tied to the biological aspects or to the psychological dynamics of intolerance.

b) Psychological dynamics have a very real capacity to influence our acts on different levels (personal, micro-social and macro-social), but it is necessary to bear in mind that in the world of human beings, the variables in play are countless and not always controllable, and for that reason, any interpretive scheme, while it may help to better comprehend the reality, must always be considered a simplification, a reduction which does not explain the complexity of each individual person.

11

c) Human situations, moreover, are always in a state of
   unstable equilibrium and for that reason must be continually
   rethought, but also "cultivated" so that they evolve in the
   desired direction.

d) Since intolerance constitutes one of the ways of relating to
   another, our analysis must take in all those dimensions
   which are implicated in human relationships, be they
   influenced by biological or psychological elements.

BIOLOGICAL ELEMENTS USEFUL FOR UNDERSTANDING THE GENESIS OF INTOLERANT BEHAVIOR

Considered from the biological point of view, the human being,
like any other animal, is dominated by the instinct of survival. Every
living being, in its evolution, has undergone a progressive transformation with respect to a "protective law" according to which only the
individual which best adapts to its surroundings, its changes, and new
requirements for defense, can survive and perpetuate the species.

With a totally unique history,[1] even the human being has
responded to the same exigencies, modifying its own brain which
little by little enriched itself with ever more complex and specialized
characteristics, absent, or commonly much reduced, in other animals. In this way, the human being was able to free itself from the
constrictions on its activity based exclusively on an instinctive reflex
to a given stimulus. The development of the brain, in fact, permits a
person to choose his own behavior based on the situation, all the
while maintaining survival as his goal.

Notwithstanding radical alterations in the nervous system and
in the life of human beings in the course of millennia, the oldest parts
of our brains are still active and indispensable to the survival of the

---

[1] To adapt, animals in the course of millennia, have modified their physiques; human
beings, instead, by means of the development of their brain, reached a point of being
able to change their environment rather than their bodies. One can speak, for that
reason, of a new way, a cultural approach, to achieving adaptation, based on the
transmission of acquired knowledge from generation to generation.

species and influence our comportment in a profound way.[2] Man, hence, acts even under the influence of these "primitive" stimuli which are especially active in situations of tension, when he feels threatened, when he identifies his "enemies."

But what is the connection between these biological dynamics and intolerant behavior?

What we have recalled is important because an intolerant attitude often is justified (and hence considered morally acceptable if not "good") by asserting that it is a matter of defense and therefore "natural," belonging to the prospect of a struggle for survival.

The theory of the evolution of conscience goes so far as to sustain that the categories of "good" and "evil" were determined in the phase of life which was still "pre-human," on the basis of the need to survive for which it is not "bad" to react to a menacing situation. It is "natural" to defend oneself from an enemy. The attitudes of intolerance would be therefore linked to a perception of the other as an enemy and to a "natural" reaction of defense. It is a purely instinctual kind of behavior whose roots reside in that remnant of our brain which is irrational, unspecialized, archaic and not evolved.[3]

> You are still of the stone and the slingshot,
> man of my times. You were in the fuselage,
> with malevolent wings, the sun-dials of death.
> I saw you in the fiery chariot, at the gallows,
> at the wheel of torture. I saw you: it was you,
> with your exact science determined to exterminate
> without love, without Christ. You killed again,
> as always, as your forefathers killed,
> as the animals who saw you for the first time.
> And this blood gives off a stench as it did on the day

---

[2] Besides the cerebral trunk (which controls vital functions maintaining the equilibrium of the fluids and temperature of the body), let us not forget the diencephalon which contributes to survival by controlling the reactions to ambient stimuli through the use of archaic defense reactions. For more on this see K. and B. Spillmann (Bibliography).

[3] The human being, in contrast with the animals, can kill also only for the pleasure in doing so; in any case, the analogy between the human desire for self-affirmation and the struggle to command, to control territory and to possess the female of the species among animals, especially among primates, still remains.

when brother said to brother: "Let's go into the fields."
And that cold, tenacious echo
reaches even to you, within your day.
Forget, O son, the clouds of blood
rising up from the earth, forget your fathers:
their tombs sink into the ashes,
the blackbirds, the wind, cover their hearts.

(Salvatore Quasimodo)

FEAR, SIMPLIFICATION, SENSE OF BELONGING

The diverse elements of the human personality can be grouped into three large categories — affective, cognitive, and social — each one of which conditions our behavior in relationships.

From the affective point of view the human being has a need to feel secure, protected from threats which can come from the surrounding environment (and hence even from other human beings).

This need of security (especially evident in little children, but persisting throughout one's life span) is strictly correlated to fear of the unknown, of what is different, of the "other." Intolerant behavior, in this sense, can be read as a form of defense.

If fear is born of the perception of the other as a threat, then also the cognitive aspects of the personality are directly involved in this process. Perception, in fact, is fundamentally a cognitive operation and it is on this basis that the other comes to be "seen" not only in visible terms but also understood, identified and recognized. In its process of knowing, man tends in fact to reduce the unknown to the known, to simplify complexity by the use of molds which are destined very often to impoverish the reality, bringing about the rise of stereotypes and unfairly attributed labels.[4] It is in this fashion that prejudices are born, that is, judgments made before really knowing all the facts.

---

[4] The qualities of this process of knowledge can be transformed also into a defect: simplification can become reductionism, the stereotype mold and the instruments of knowledge can be converted into obstacles to a more profound understanding.

We asked some Italian and Polish high school students to define certain populations by listing ten characteristics for each. Here are examples of some of their responses: Germans are blond, tall, mustached, cold, hard, beer drinkers. . . The Senegalese are dark, dirty, poor, with big lips, no diplomas, no desire to work. . . Russians are communists, without personality, pale, proud, cold and calculating, traditionalists, imperialists, and so forth.

These examples are clearly the fruit of uncalled for simplification due to limited experience and superficial knowledge, often not even direct, of persons who belong to such nationalities. The individual differences disappear behind some traits which seem dominant, but which are not necessarily present; the real individual cedes his place to the stereotype and this, once established, is very difficult to eradicate, along with the consequent prejudices. Labels are easy, they avoid the effort to go deeper. The stereotype of the other, be he a foreigner or different from the model of reference (basically it's enough to be a baby, a woman, a sick old man, poor, atheistic, to be different), is often tied to a sense of disadvantage which at times turns into fear. If the one who is different is thus a threat, right away there is an intolerant reaction, one of self-defense, protection, estrangement, isolation.

Even the social dimension of an individual contributes to orienting his relationship with others: either because the mental representations of the other are often the fruit of a "collective imagination," or because each person bears within himself the need to belong to a group with which he can identify. Besides having a personal identity, in fact, each one of us also has a social identity (it might be more correct to speak of several social identities): one's last name, which indicates the family to which one belongs, constitutes only a very elementary example, since one is considered by others not only in virtue of his origin, but also in virtue of the role he plays in society (worker, businessman, professional. . .). We can for that reason say that our identity is made up of concentric circles: in the innermost ones we find our most intimate being; little by little as we move to the outside, characteristics common to us and to others increase.

So, for example, if for my friends I am "Valentino," to others
I may be "Father Salvoldi," for others, a priest, and for yet others a
writer, an Italian, a European, a white man, and so forth.
Evidently my identity varies according to the person with
whom I am speaking and according to how well he knows me. The
discourse is logically valid even for those whom I meet and identify
on the basis of that which I consider to be their affiliations.

It is clear, at this point, that the sense of belonging can, along
with the other elements mentioned, favor or block relationships with
one's neighbor: it can in fact become a barrier, generate divisions, or
bring to light points held in common. The greater the narrowness (not
necessarily in size) of the group to which I feel I belong, the greater
will be my mistrust, my lack of esteem, my fear of the other, seen
again as a threat, as someone different, as an enemy, and so forth.

Albert Einstein was fleeing from Nazi Germany by train. At a
control point, the police asked him this question: "To what race do
you belong?" "To the human race," was his reply. It's easy to see how
the sense of belonging was wider and more open in Einstein as
compared with that of the closed and threatening German police.[5]

---

[5] Today we live in a society which, at least virtually, has abolished all frontiers: every
part of the globe is easy accessible thanks to the most rapid and modern means of
transport. To those who can not travel, television brings into the house the world of
others, proving that our life is lived in the context of great complexity. Science and
technology have made it so that each one of us is called to specialize in a little part of a
work which can be controlled from beginning to end only with great difficulty. All of
us, besides, feel more threatened in our identity, if not in our very survival, by "others"
because the distance between human beings has been enormously reduced and the
potential for destruction has increased disproportionately.

All of this can not but generate stress and a desire to simplify reality in order to better
comprehend it (cognitive dimension). The close proximity of many "others" drives man
to close himself in and to identify with groups which are more restricted and limited
(social dimension), in which he can feel himself to be a protagonist but also secure and
protected (affective dimension). For that reason it is evident how easy it is to incite
reactions of intolerance when the burden of tension is so high as to require a much more
elevated capacity to control one's own behavior.

Far from wanting to justify intolerant conduct through these reflections, we do want,
however, to throw light on the very real difficulties which are met in this field in order,
then, to seek with greater vigor, the means and the ideal incentives which will allow us
to continue on the path to tolerance, within and outside ourselves.

"When you see that your goal is a long way off, start walking." (A Chinese proverb)

— III —
Towards A Belonging That Is Universal

The path we propose, after having analyzed the psycho-social reality of intolerance, will lead us to the discovery of several ways of "building" tolerance. We realize the struggle of a course such as this, but we maintain that reflection can help every adult person to change his own attitude and comportment vis-a-vis others, to the point of being born again to the joy of friendly relationships, of tolerance, and of solidarity.

In his book *L'Unità, speranza di vita*, Brother Roger, spiritual leader of the ecumenical monastic community of Taizé, presents the thesis that the unity of the person ought to be the condition for unity among all human beings:

> Every search for unity between human beings implies first of all that this unity be accomplished within the self. . . Then, to the extent in which inner unity averts the disintegration which threatens us every day, it becomes possible to work for the unity of all men and to ardently await the visible unit of all Christians in one Church. . . Divided in himself, man is also divided with regard to his neighbor. Because of the lack of unity within his person, very often in the most intimate depths of the self, there arises the need to affirm the self in opposition to others, to separate that which ought to be united (pp. 15-16).

The ecumenical community of Taizé is living testimony to the will to be "one," according to the spirit of the Gospels (see especially the Gospel of St. John), to overcome the differences which become barriers, to seek that which unites and not that which divides. It is a living example of tolerance and solidarity that ought to be a concrete example for everyone and not only for those who have opted for a monastic way of life.

Inner unity (peace of soul) thus seems to be a fundamental quality for achieving the goal which we have set for ourselves, yet it has to do also with an achievement never fully realized, always threatened as it is by the evil spirit of division. (Is this not perhaps the etymological significance behind the term "devil," one who divides, who renders useless the work of the sower?)

It is not easy to live peaceably: too many messages impose on us the model of the winner. Christ, instead, speaks of the power of weakness, of the cross (1 Cor 1:18). Only those who have in their hearts a spirit of peace can succeed in conquering the spiral of violence, can demonstrate and dispense true joy.

In practice, however, this road necessitates constant surveillance over our way of acting, to allow us to arrive at a habitual or usual way of behaving based on tolerance. We hope to point out here some aspects which require special attention.

1. We have spoken of the survival instinct as a force that can bring us to be suspicious of others, to see them as enemies and which can induce us to close in on ourselves, to defend ourselves even by attacking others. This succeeds, though, only because we see survival in individual and not so much in collective terms. Today, however, we are called to rethink the future of humanity, beyond our own personal destiny. The actual situation involves a precarious political equilibrium (always at the planetary level) characterized by a high destructive potential. The effects of world conflicts (even played out in lands far away, e.g. the Gulf war) have dramatic repercussions on the entire population of the planet.

If we want to survive, therefore, it is indispensable to think of a common survival, which involves all humanity, even in its weakest links. It is this survival instinct alone which can save us, which alone is worth fighting for.

2. The need to feel secure and protected is another element guiding our comportment. To constructively orient this impulse means to educate ourselves to the trust and understanding of others,

to live in empathy with those whom we meet (to place ourselves in the shoes of another with little or no emotional participation) and to place our trust in persons rather than in things as the object of our affections.

In this way even the self-esteem of each one can be founded on the knowledge of self, of one's own interior life and not so much on the possession of material goods.

3. As far as the danger of arbitrary simplifications (which are born of the need to shed light on the chaos of the multiplicity of stimuli which the world sends our way) is concerned, an in-depth study and reflection on one's own and others' experience and attention to their various aspects is necessary.

What counts most is to be aware of the imperfections in these simplifications, useful but not always able to render reason out of complexity; but still more important is the awareness — united with the acceptance — of one's own limits, even intellectual. Only in this case can the arrogance of those convinced that they possess the whole truth fall. To know one's own incapacity to penetrate the most profound secrets of the universe permits one, in fact, to maintain an attitude of openness before the mystery called "man."

"Now we see as in a mirror, darkly; but then we shall see face to face. Now we know in an imperfect manner, but then we shall know perfectly, even as we are known" (1 Cor 13:12).

4. Let us recall, besides, the need to have a social identity, to feel part of a group: to advance toward tolerance means in this case to enlarge as much as possible the "sphere of the we," the reference group with which we feel akin.

First, however, in order to pass from the individual to the universal dimension, it is necessary to understand the value of belonging to a group. If the group lives with an open and available spirit, the experience becomes a valid instrument of introduction to the universal sphere. If, instead, it is lived as a place in which the "I" of the individual must find its total satisfaction, then it becomes a means which foments intolerance, insofar as it is an expression of collective egoism.[1] The transition of the individual to the community, from the particular to the universal, requires the passage from "I" to "You," open to "We," to the group which expresses an authentic personalism.

The group is healthy if personalism is lived as the relationship of "I-You" projected towards the "We." (God is a community.)

Without the transcendent dimension, the passage of the "I" to the group becomes the very poisonous formula for egoism.

To seek oneself in a group open to the transcendent does not mean to renounce or deny one's roots, but rather to have full awareness of one's being, of one's own belonging to the human race. We have absolutely no intention of denying the need for approval, nor do we espouse the abolition of differences; it rather interests us more to enrich ourselves with that which is the common patrimony of humanity in all its multiplicity of expressions.

When you come to think of it, the ancients understood that "all that is human is mine," and today, when we hear the bell which announces the passing of another, we love to repeat, in the words of John Donne: "Don't ask for whom the bell tolls: it tolls for thee!" ("Devotions Upon Emergent Occasions").

In another's destiny, in fact, I can also read my own future: a future characterized by respect, harmony, and the joy of living, or a future filled with tension, mistrust, and useless rancor. An ethic of respect for others, in their distinctive ethnic, cultural, religious or political aspects, must guide our lives. Basic to this must be an esteem for the other equal to that which we have for ourselves, free of all preconceptions and prejudices which offend the most intimate identity of the person. As human beings, we have a common destiny. Our "common home," then, can not have borders which are too narrow: the planet must be our home and its survival is indispensable to our own, to that of all men and women of whatever color, culture, or profession of faith.

---

[1] An example of collective egoism is to be had in those cultures in which to rob another belonging to one's own group is considered a sin, while it is considered heroism to rob from another tribe.

To each of us is entrusted a specific job. But to all of us together has been given the responsibility for the care of this earth ("It is the only one we have," was the way a slogan of a few years back put it) and of its inhabitants.

5. Last of all let us mention the theme of the new dimension and the new dynamic in pluralism.

In the so-called primitive cultures, all entered into the same *Weltanschauung*, into the same world view. Customs and ideas were inspired by the same myths and the same traditions. Normally such a situation continued down through the ages without anyone having the sensation of being hemmed in, since no one knew any other *Weltanschauung* or model of society. But today as contact with other world views becomes more frequent, many realities which had seemed certain now seem uncertain.[2] In other words, in primitive societies, individuals could, yes, place themselves into conflict with their traditions and their society, but they understood that in so doing they set themselves apart and remained without any support. The new pluralism instead has brought with it not only that the individual might think for himself but that entire groups might also set themselves up independently with their own cultural, political and religious choices.

Pluralism finds its modern political expression in democracy, in which, at least in theory, diverse groups enjoy the same chance, while to all is guaranteed freedom of expression within the limits of the law. But, to function correctly, political pluralism must respect other forms of pluralism and understand their significance and their purpose.[3]

---

[2] Cf. I. Magli, in D. Basili, *Pluralismo*, Rome, 1976, pp. 194-198.

[3] In this regard, Pope Pius XII spoke in 1944 of the challenge posed by democracy if it is to be called true and sound. An authentic democracy, he said, requires a populace that is aware of its rights and duties, capable of giving itself rulers who are equal to the task, that is, gifted with a "clear understanding of the ends assigned by God to every human society, combined with the profound sense of the sublime duties of social work." Only under these conditions, in fact, can those to whom power is entrusted fulfill their own obligations "with the awareness of their own responsibility, with that objectivity, impartiality, generosity and incorruptibility without which a democratic government would find it difficult to obtain the respect, confidence and support of the better part of the populace" (*Addresses and Radio Messages of His Holiness Pius XII*, Vol. VI, p. 237).

The aspect of pluralism which most interests us here is the new way of arriving at the truth, one which the mass media makes particular use of in its approach to truth.

According to the Englishman Sir Hugh Greene, Director General of Programming for the BBC, pluralism, to have any possibility of surviving, "must be so able as to know how to combine the most profound skepticism with the most profound faith, the obligation to be tolerant within the widest possible freedom of expression."[4]

Pluralism begins with the attitude of Socrates: "I know nothing except the fact of my ignorance" (Diogenes Laertius, *Lives of Eminent Philosophers*, Bk II, sec. 32), which for him implied a tireless search for truth. John Milton expressed the same idea: "Where there is much desire to learn, there of necessity will be much arguing, much writing, many opinions; for opinion in good men is but knowledge in the making" (*Areopagitica* [1664]).[5] In Socrates we have a person who sought the truth. In modern pluralistic society, the search for truth has become ever more a collective search, and that brings with it on one side the enjoyment of freedom, and on the other the birth of conflicts.

Pluralism is healthy if the opinions of other persons and groups are taken seriously and if no one tries to stifle the others with pressure or constraints. Pluralism presupposes a culture in which each group wants "to learn and to unlearn," in which all hunger to know themselves and others better in such a way that, by means of their common effort, they may arrive at a more profound and broader understanding of the truth.

Pluralism does not by any means signify an anarchy of ideas and a society without structure. Democracy need reciprocal respect between human beings and an agreement on certain basic values. Tolerance does not imply a neutrality of thought, but every group will mature its vision and experience in the co-reflection of all, in common respect for the rules agreed upon. Sir Hugh Greene ex-

---

[4] Sir Hugh Greene, *The Conscience of the Programme Director*, London, 1965, p. 5.

[5] Cited in H. Greene, *op. cit.*, p. 5.

presses this clearly: "If in the daily transmission of public life the BBC tries to follow the highest levels of impartiality, there are certain sectors in which it is neither neutral nor impartial. That happens when there are conflicts of opinion for or against basic moral values such as truthfulness, justice, liberty, compassion, tolerance. Nor do I think that we ought to be impartial before such things as racism or extremist kinds of political creeds. To be too good a 'democrat' in such questions could open the way to the destruction of democracy itself. I believe that a healthy democracy doesn't have to avoid taking a stand regarding what it will never permit if it wants to survive."[6]

An authentic pluralistic culture presupposes and demands a sense of solidarity and respect for the dignity and conscience of each person. It excludes both extreme individualism and totalitarian tendencies. In a culture and in an authentically pluralistic society, the men and women who pretend to have a monopoly on truth and who preoccupy themselves more with safety than with the courageous and sincere search for truth, will have a difficult life.

---

[6] *Ibid.*, p. 12.

Persons and Values:
Towards a Philosophy of Tolerance

The human being who is shaped through reason and relationships can be defined as "one who has the will to love and to be loved." One becomes fully human through the capacity to create a bond with God, with oneself, with others, with creation, and with history.

In modern thought — with René Descartes — the person, insofar as he relates to himself, is reduced to an "I" with a conscience. Immanuel Kant, while accepting this concept of modern thought, poses the problem of the rapport with others as characterizing the person. The "other," according to this German philosopher, always has the dignity of being an end in itself and can never be used as a means.

But it is phenomenology, above all, which places the accent on the concept of person as hetero-relationship (one in relationship with others). Max Scheler defines the person as one having an affinity with the world: the "I" is essentially in rapport with that which is external to itself; the individual has an affinity with society, the body with its surroundings. Martin Heidegger bases his existential analysis on the concept of the human person's "being at home" in his rapport with the world.

From these presuppositions a concept of the person evolved which was no longer founded on the "I." The social sciences understand by "person" the individual endowed with a social status, who is characterized by a series of interpersonal relationships.

In contemporary philosophical thought, the affinity between person and society is based on the personalism of Emmanuel Mounier, Jacques Maritain and the Frankfurt school which was preoccupied not so much in giving a definition to the person, as it was in safeguarding the dignity of the human being. Recently Martin Buber and Emmanuel Levinas have insisted a great deal on the value of the "I-You" relationship in view of a purely transcendental "We." Affinity with others — according to these two philosophers — is valid to the extent in which the "You" includes God, and the "We" is an expression of the family of God. That "you" which only serves to momentarily exalt does not free. While the "you" of the poor and the indigent, the "you" which seeks and brings one to a universal love prepares for authentic transcendence, for the transcendent "You," for the "Other" who is God.[1]

Assisted by these philosophical currents, ethics and morality are faced with the problem of interpersonal relationships, of their justification, of the basis for respect for the other as a person and, consequently, for "tolerance."

Seeking to overcome the idea that an affinity with others serves only in view of coexistence (instrumental rapport), one feels the need to give a foundation to the intuition that the person is defined as one in relationship with a "you," with others, with the "Other" in the absolute sense, God (a valid relationship only if the reciprocal subjectivity is respected and the mutual possibility of fulfilling oneself in freedom is favored).

The validity of a relationship is measured by its capacity to involve persons in a mutual gift of self, in a way that every encounter

---

[1] Martin Buber was an authentic prophet because he never exalted his people at the expense of others. He understood well that the election of his people was framed in the context of the Servant of Yahweh. Israel was chosen insofar as it was the incarnation of the famous servant of God to whom it was promised: "It is too little, he says, for you to be my servant, to raise up the tribes of Jacob, and restore the survivors of Israel; I will make you a light to the nations that my salvation may reach to the ends of the earth" (Is 49:6).

Emmanuel Levinas followed the lines of Buber insisting more on God as the Other who has a right over every man. To this transcendent Other is led the "other," the poor, the indigent, the enemy. If one only loves his friends, he can fall into a form of narrow-minded egoism. If one loves those who are different and who require to be recognized as a "you," this love is already an immersion in transcendence.

serves to generate love.[2] From the definition of God as love, from the revelation of Christ as life given as gift for the salvation of all, derives — for the Christian — the obligation to consider the person as a value in him or herself, but also as one with whom one has an inter-human affinity, as giver and gift, as one in whom one searches for the divine in daily life.

The Church speaks of love more than it does of tolerance. However, at the bottom of its social teaching there are substantially two truths:

1. The Christian must respect every human being because the person is sovereign, free, and carries within itself the image of the Creator;
2. The human being is fulfilled in relationship with another, with all others, and in first place with God. "Insofar as man by his very nature stands completely in need of life in society, he is and ought to be the beginning, the subject, and the object of every social organization. Life in society is not something accessory to man himself: through his dealings with others, through mutual service, and through fraternal dialogue, man develops all his talents and becomes able to rise to his destiny" (*Gaudium et spes*, 25).

THE VALUE OF THE HUMAN BEING AND "VALUES"

To deepen the concept of the value of the person, it is necessary to reflect above all on the significance of "moral values." Instinc-

---

[2] The pastoral constitution of the Second Vatican Council has this scope in mind: "Furthermore, the Lord Jesus, when praying to the Father 'that they may all be one. . . even as we are one' (Jn 17:21-22), has opened up new horizons closed to human reason by implying that there is a certain parallel between the union existing among the divine persons and the union of the sons of God in truth and love. It follows, then, that if man is the only creature on earth that God has wanted for its own sake, man can fully discover his true self only in a sincere giving of himself" (*Gaudium et spes*, 24).

tively we are led to appreciate actions or choices which value others more: attention given to a poor person, fidelity even to one who has betrayed, consistency in expressing one's ideas even when it turns to one's own disadvantage. Values are at work which help one be more human, more communicative, better, which solicit our conscience, obliging us to react and opt for a higher good, to the advantage of all.

The sense of values and of what is good can be felt by every human being, of whatever culture to which he or she may belong: it has a universal character. Can one, therefore, speak of the existence of a "human nature"? Are human beings essentially the same in all times and places? Do the same values exist for all of them? For centuries it was thought that the essence of being human was unchangeable, deducing from this laws valid for all. But, over the last two centuries, this general trend of thought has changed. Now more attention is placed on the historical character of the person, rooted in a specific culture, time and locale. Because the creature we call a human being is a reality with a spiritual nature, it can no longer be considered in a static way, defined once and for all.

Who are you? "Someone, no one, a hundred thousand. . . ."

The human sciences, in dialog with one another, have placed in evidence the complexity of the human being, of its nature, of the diverse ways in which it fulfills its principal aspirations. Granted that all agree that one "must do good and avoid evil," there is a great deal of dissent over determining what is good and what is evil.

Beyond the different interpretations given to the same reality, however, there is also always something which unites human beings: their differences from the animal world, the use of language, the ability to sense intuitively that, if they want to survive on the face of the earth, they will have to make use of the initial intuitions from which probably every ethical discourse originated: "You shall not kill"; "You shall not commit incest" (You will be open to other groups).[3]

The persistence of something which unites human beings,

---

[3] See S. Colombo, *La morale cos'è?* in *Communità Redona*, January 1993, insert i-xvi.

beyond the variations in culture, came to be called with the passage of time the "natural law." Today this term, fallen largely into disuse, has given place to a kind of "universal consent," based on the study of the needs of human beings, both at the personal as well as the social-collective levels.

To survive, or better, to be able to live with dignity, human beings must agree on essential values which permit respect for their bodily existence and which safeguard their spiritual and rational life as well. Some fundamental ethical values can be expressed in these terms:

1. To the good of one's bodily existence, life must be declared sacred; it is to be preserved intact from conception to natural death. (The commandment, "You shall not kill," then, is valid even for war which cannot be justified, either on the rational — see the theme on nonviolent defence — or on the moral level: the 5th commandment and the teaching of Christ which tells us to love even our enemies are always valid);
2. For the good of the individual it is indispensable to safe-guard all that would permit one to live with dignity: "You shall not rob";
3. For the good of life in community, the human creature needs to be esteemed, honored, and must never be the object of calumny: "You shall not lie";
4. For the good of the human being as a rational creature, the search for truth, liberty, and God must be favored (the first three commandments).

These human rights, which touch one's corporal and rational nature, founded on an ethical plane, become, for those who believe, expressions of the will of God. And so we have the Ten Command-ments and the moral laws registered in the Oriental juridical codes already in force several centuries before Christ.

On this substantial structure of the human being, on his ethical and social needs, were based the formulation of human rights, solemnly promulgated — and accepted by most States — only following the Second World War. This universal consensus is indispensable for coexistence as human beings and for the maturation of each individual human being who, feeling himself ever more threatened in the precariousness of life by the lack of space, work and hope, tends to become aggressive and violent, to turn in on himself, to insist on his own rights and deny those of the others. We can affirm here that moral values express all those things which are imposed on human beings to allow them to live a dignified existence, to seek the good, the beautiful and the true, as a possibility which broadens ever more their horizons and their space to be free.

The first of all these human values, in an absolute sense, is the person, who is important in himself, by the simple fact of his existence. The person is not important for what he owns or for the position he occupies, but only because he is! For the believer in Christ, the greatest is not the one who holds the highest posts in the state or ecclesiastical hierarchy, but the least, the one who loves the most.

Besides the importance which he has in himself, a person receives an added value when he is held in consideration, is esteemed, appreciated, sought after, liked and loved by those closest to him, by his family, his friends, society. Having a sense of worth in his own eyes and in the collective esteem of others helps him to develop to the highest his own potential and to give himself to others. This way of life facilitates the circulation, production and multiplication of values by means of works of "justice, peace and the care of creation." Through action (the natural outpouring of a mind which reasons and of a heart which excludes nothing and no one) the person expresses himself as a gift and releases into the world an added spirit to the advantage of the progressive realization of the potential value of each and every human being.

These values, however, do not arise at the same time in every part of the world: history, culture, time and diverse places see to it that the circulation of values are neither homogeneous nor uncertain.

Values can come up against obstacles that are not inconsequential and can create conflicts which themselves need to be analyzed and evaluated.

THE EVALUATION OF CONFLICTS

Conformism is not the life ideal of a mature person, nor should it be characteristic of the Christian who, to be such, is continuously called to take on the mantle of the prophet, to be the voice critical of every injustice and, if necessary, to go against the current. The social order, in fact, is not a reality given once and for always, but is a dynamic unfolding of possibilities, which involves the mature person, inviting him to use discernment and prudence (virtues which consist in weighing all the possibilities in order, then, to select the best).

A prophetic spirit, insight and discernment, like liberty and courage (the art of plain speaking, without half measures, going right to the heart of every question), are indispensable virtues for confronting a reality full of conflicts which must not be demonized but faced and resolved positively.

The Golden Age never did exist on earth and it is not realistic to think that perfect harmony can ever be achieved in our society. Nor is it right to hold that it is possible to apply, in dealing with diverse social groups, the kind of rapport existing between two friends. The diversity of character, temperament, ideas, and interests leads to a divergence which can be stimulating in view of overcoming difficulties. To overcome obstacles along the way it is helpful to put our higher potentials into act and challenge ourselves to reach ever higher goals. In a dialectic mentality, the antithesis is used as a stimulus to go further, to arrive at a synthesis: this, in its turn, sees another obstacle in its way which, overcome, leads to a new synthesis and so on.

Before seeking to evaluate obstacles and social conflicts, the person who wants to mature and to be able to draw from himself "things old yet ever new," puts himself to the test in situations which are particularly difficult: the "great" confront the desert, the solitude of the mountaintop, the fatigue of study, the mortification of their bodies, the exercise of the memory and the practice of all the virtues.

In many African tribes, boys who have reached the age of puberty are sent in groups into the forest to learn to become men, facing a hostile environment where the law of the strongest rules, and adapting themselves to eating very little when food is scarce and to eating much when the catch goes well, showing real and true proof of courage.

It is what even Jesus did who, according to the concise and telling Gospel of Mark "was driven by the Spirit out into the desert. He stayed in the desert for forty days being tempted by Satan. He was with the wild animals, and angels served him" (1:12-13). The wild beasts are a symbol of all adversity, the angels represent aspirations to eternal values. Christ as man grows and makes of himself a bridge between heaven and earth, overcoming human limits and contradictions, seeking help from on High.

As far as social conflicts are concerned, the person must take a stance between two extreme situations, that which is ingenuously pacific (pacifist) and that which radicalizes the conflict. One cannot pretend not to see the tension: the true non-violent pacifist is one who denounces the hypocrisy of those who cloak over tensions and accept a sepulchral peace; he is one who places in evidence the injustices suffered by the poorest of the poor, and who stigmatizes social evil. Such a person does not make conflict a way of life, as if tension were the very principle of life itself (Marxist dialectic), but when faced with an incipient conflict, by means of dialog, goes in search of solutions which are realistic and shared by both contending parties.

The nonviolent, in other words, know that conflicts are not resolved through moralistic discourses, which seek to make the persons feel guilty, as if the evil of the world were due to the ill will of some individuals. On earth there exist unjust systems and sinful structures which must be opposed because in a system of oppression persons can never extricate themselves, or free themselves, or fulfill themselves.[4] Given the existence of unjust and iniquitous structures, the attitude of those who preach that, for a better world it would be sufficient for a person to be converted and become a saint, is mystifying. Saints can contribute enormously to human progress, so long as men and women of good will commit themselves to reforming unfair structures, to bringing about justice on earth, to making the most of differences. In a word, to create and promote a culture of tolerance.

FIDELITY TO THE PERSON

Every human being, who is called to live with his fellow human beings, is also called to be a gift to the other. The culture of tolerance is born of fidelity to the person. The other can be understood as a rival, one who robs you of vital space, who defiles and makes trouble: therefore an enemy to annihilate? But aggression and violence create a chain of hate and war, with the risk that humanity itself will come apart and disappear from the face of the earth. The ancient Romans had already understood, at least theoretically, that it would be better to consider the "other" not as an enemy but as a guest (*"Non hostis, sed hospes"*).

Christ, then, explicitly said that we must do evil to no one, instead that we were to love everyone, even those who assume the role of an enemy. The Christian is always called to convert hate into love, to disarm revenge with pardon, to pass from a negative state of conflict to a positive one of acceptance of all.

To accept another is the same as to receive him not as a being who serves our own interest and with whom we can freely dispose, but as a person towards whom we become "responsible." Many

---

[4] Pope John Paul II spoke very clearly about this in his encyclical *Sollicitudo rei socialis*. Among these sinful structures the entire military apparatus is also to be included. For more on this theme see V. Salvoldi, *Struttura militare, struttura di peccato?* in *Arcobaleno di pace*, n. 10 (1993), pp. 23ff. and B. Häring - V. Salvoldi, *Nonviolenza, per osare la pace*, Ed. Messaggero, Padua 1993.

glances, even when not accompanied by words or gestures of any kind, are at the same time an invocation and a gift. To accept another is to make him "be" and in the process to enrich ourselves. To refuse another is to abandon him to himself, depriving him and ourselves of that love which only grows through reciprocal giving. The true acceptance of a person is manifested in the ability to forgive, in the will to forget wrongs undergone, in the willingness to search together for harmony (cf. Ac 4:32-35) and for that love which is never offered in vain, but which multiplies while it is being shared with more and more persons.

Tolerant acceptance requires a willingness to enter into a diversity of opinions, thought and faith, and to have recourse to dialog to overcome error, in the awareness than no one possesses a monopoly on Truth and that Truth is presented in a many-sided way. Tolerance is, then, the virtue of a strong person, who knows how to be patient, who does not harden his heart, who accepts life with serene courage and is gradually liberated from the presumption of being better than others and from the prejudices which block any dialog and hinder the search to create meaningful encounters.

Fidelity to the person, expressed through tolerance, does not imply a blind acceptance of his limits, nor agreement with his errors. The one who errs is to be understood; the error is to be corrected. Above all when one assumes a pedagogical role vis-à-vis young people, one must be demanding, capable of setting forth highly elevated goals, disposed to accompany them, setting the pace for the weakest as when one climbs a mountain. All the while, though, the fundamental attitude, expressed in a concise way by the apostle Paul, must remain clear: "To live the truth in love" (Eph 4:15).

Without question we must love everyone, but love must be based on a relationship of sincerity and on the search for that truth which sets one free and renders one able to free others (cf. *Gaudium et spes*, 28).

— V —

From Particularism to Universalism:
A Biblical Approach

The concept of tolerance, understood as respect for the person as a human being endowed with rights and duties, is the result of the re-flections of modern times. We cannot, therefore, have recourse to the Bible for its justification. In fact, the Old Testament presents a long series of items which indicate how very intolerant most of the people in those times were. In the New Testament, the word "tolerance" is to be found only once, and there it refers to God (cf. Rm 2:4 NJB).

The concept, instead, can be deduced from the attitude of Christ as well as from his teaching.

We want to approach the Bible for the sole purpose of deepen-ing our understanding of:

— the tension between ethnocentrism and universalism;
— the significance of the term "patience" and its synonyms, among which there is "tolerance"[1];
— the invitation of Christ not to uproot the weeds but to be merciful as his heavenly Father is merciful.

THE ELECTION OF ISRAEL AND UNIVERSAL SALVATION

Against Babylon, which wanted to lay waste to Israel, the psalmist says: "Happy the man who shall seize and smash your little

---

[1] Even as far as the biblical texts are concerned we find the idea expressed in the introduction once again: for tolerance one understands the acceptance of the person, not the courage and the strength of soul to endure the weight of a difficult situation.

35

ones against the rock!" (137:9). But there is another psalmist who proclaims: "The Lord is good to all and compassionate towards all his works" (145:9). At first glance it would seem that ethnocentrism, the exclusive election of Israel, prevails. In reality, when God chooses one he does not exclude the other, does not love less those not chosen. On the contrary, he gives his gifts (charisms) to a person or group in light of the common good. The choice of a people or of a person is a sign of an unmerited and gratuitous gift, given to an individual which becomes a "blessing for all."

We can understand the passage from particularism to universalism only if we do not limit ourselves to individual facts or specific expressions which, taken in themselves, might even scandalize, but if we keep in mind the history behind the biblical revelation, its incarnation, its tension towards the fulness of time and towards the fulness of joy on the last day when "God will be all in all."

Alongside the history of intolerance in the Bible there is a thread which helps the reader to pass from particularism to universalism, to trace a history of salvation offered to the whole human race. We limit ourselves to some significant examples:

(a) Adam (*Hà-adam*) is the universal man, "clay which thinks," saint and sinner. In him we see all Israel, an image of God, masculine and feminine. Because his sin is also our own, that of the whole human race, each one of us feels the weight of that fault on our own shoulders, as a terrible burden which keeps us from accomplishing the good and avoiding the evil which is oftentimes so seductive.

(b) In the call of Abraham (Genesis 12) all the families of the earth were blessed. This man, Abraham, was uprooted from his land and led to a place unknown to him ("without knowing where he was going" [Heb 11:8]), to hear in a foreign land the human word of God, to seek his own identity, his own visage as a new human creature in comparison with other faces, other cultures, other religions. In a foreign land, Abraham will become rich in the eyes of God who asked him to leave everything. He will become a believer in the exhausting anticipation of heaven's answer, for a hundred years putting his faith in the promise that his progeny would be "more numerous than the stars of the sky." He will become the symbol of hope in experiencing the power of God as a live seed in the dead womb of Sarah. He will become a father in the fullest sense of the word when he will have gotten beyond the idea that God wills human sacrifice in order to be placated. The biblical author in this passage does not exalt blind obedience to God, but that predisposition to realize his loving plan and his effort to lead the believer from a human way of thinking to one based on love, to a life in which one serves, to the concept of gift as "being for others."[2]

(c) The election of Israel (cf. Dt 4:7) and its march toward the Promised Land did not come about through the merits of this people, but because it was the smallest of all the nations. In fact, this is the logic of God: to choose those who are not and make them to be, for the advantage of the whole human race (cf. Dt 7:7-8).

(d) Israel is called to be an intermediary between God and other peoples: "I will make you a light to the nations that my salvation may reach to the ends of the earth" (Is 49:6).

(e) The prophets speak of foreigners used by God to make Israel return to reason: Assyria is called the "scourge of God" and Babylon is "the hammer of the Lord." Even pagan nations must submit to the judgment of God and hence comport themselves according to his laws, acting with justice. For all nations there is the possibility of conversion, of reaching the mountain of the Lord, where there will be peace for everyone (cf. Is 2:1-5, Mi 4:1-3; Is 60). Out of all the nations, and from among all those who

---

[2] In this context Isaac becomes a figure of Christ in his predisposition to be sacrificed in order not to displease God, but to place himself at the service of the survival of the new humanity. A healthy nonviolent person is one who prefers to be killed rather than to kill, because he understands the weakness of the enemy, feels compassion and takes upon himself their limitations.

will reach Zion, the Lord will select priests and Levites (cf.
Is 60:21).

(f) The book of Jonah is particularly interesting (valid as a
"narrative theology") to understand the theme of tolerance.
God shows himself as the Father of all and chooses a
prophet of Israel to save Nineveh. The prophet flees from
God who follows him and forces him to prophesy in a
foreign city. God shows his love for all the people and
reproves the narrow-mindedness, the "myopia" of Jonah,
the mistaken conviction that Israel was the only people
loved by the Lord. God cares for all and hence the prophet
must imitate the Lord and feel himself to be responsible for
the well-being and salvation of all people. If God shows
himself to be merciful with the prophet (to the point of
causing a gourd plant to spring up and shade him from the
sun), then his servant must exercise the same mercy towards
other human beings in need of help, comfort and guidance
so as not to fall into error or sin.

(g) Above all, it was Deutero-Isaiah who opened the eyes of the
Israelites to a truly universal horizon: God, the Lord of all
things and peoples, will make use of the Persian King Cyrus
as a kind of "messiah" (cf. Is 45:4, 9-13; 46:9-11; 48:12-
15).

(h) The Servant of Yahweh, from the poems dedicated to him,
is described as gifted with a universal mission: he is called
to bring justice to the nations (cf. Is 42:1), salvation to the
ends of the earth (cf. 49:6), and to receive in homage
multitudes of people (cf. 52:5; 53:12).

(i) Malachi seems to allude to the possibility that every cult
offered to God with a sincere heart in every part of the
globe gives glory to the Lord: "From the rising of the sun,
even to its setting, my name is great among the nations; and
everywhere they bring sacrifice to my name, and a pure
offering; for great is my name among the nations, says the
Lord of hosts" (1:11).

(j) It would be useful to analyze the Wisdom books to unearth the interest which the biblical authors had for the human being as such, his preoccupation to understand the meaning of existence, thus deepening the fundamental themes of the philosophy and culture of all human beings. It suffices to cite the books of Qoheleth and Job. Also the Song of Songs, with its sublime poetic component, has a universalistic message, which can be summarized in the intuition: "Where there is love, there is God." In this poem, there is no need to name the Lord: speaking of love, one wants to avoid repeating oneself, since love is God. This will be the central theme of the letter of the evangelist St. John.

GOD, PATIENT AND MERCIFUL

The human being, radically poor, places his confidence in God, awaiting his assistance and trusting in his patience and mercy. According to the Bible, the human being learns patience, and with it all that can be expressed by its synonyms (perseverance, constancy, strength of soul, magnanimity and tolerance), looking to God, the hope of his people, to him who is "kind, good, merciful, patient, slow to anger," and so forth.

Human existence is always threatened by grave difficulties which bring the human being to feel limited, contingent, almost suspended in nothingness. Faced with such a situation, with the Greeks he may ask not for the help of the gods but for resignation; with the Buddhist and Hindu cultures, for ataraxy, undisturbed peace, the extinction of all desires. These are not the biblical perspective. The Word invites the believer to hope in God and to acquire the virtue of patience, to live clinging to the Lord, right up to the very end.

Moses, hidden in the cleft of the rock, wants to see the face of God, wants to know something more of the divine. To him, even if he will only be allowed to see the back of the cloak of God, will be

given the sublime revelation of God's essence: "The Lord passed
before him and proclaimed, 'The Lord, the Lord, a God merciful and
gracious, slow to anger, and abounding in steadfast love and faithful-
ness'" (Ex 34:6).

You cannot improvise the virtue of patience, nor keep it only
for the moment of trial: like hope, it is a fragile virtue, like a flower
which must be cultivated over time. Its roots are trust in the Lord:
"Wait for the Lord with courage; be stouthearted and wait for the
Lord" (Ps 27:14). "Hope does not disappoint, because the love of
God has been poured out into our hearts through the Holy Spirit that
has been given to us" (Rm 5:5). The ultimate foundation for patience
is the presence of God in us who generates the charity from which
hope is born; at the basis of all, however, there is faith, the virtue
through which we make ourselves completely dependent on God.

To expect all from God is not a sign of passivity, inertia, or
resignation, but is rather an explicit profession of faith: "Those who
hope in the Lord will renew their strength, they will soar as with
eagles' wings; they will run and not grow weary, walk and not grow
faint" (Is 40:31).

Wrath and grace are the two poles which characterize the
revelation of the "face" of God, who likes to show himself to be
intransigent, unapproachable, awesome, and just, but who at the
same time, knows how to be as tender as a mother who presses her
baby to her cheek, as lenient as a father who encourages the first
faltering steps of his child. Wrath and grace are placed in evidence in
a text more than once re-echoed in the pages of the Old Testament:
"The Lord shows his steadfast love for thousands, forgiving iniquity
and transgression and sin, but who will by no means clear the guilty,
visiting the iniquity of the fathers upon the children and the children's
children, to the third and the fourth generation" (Ex 34:7).

The "wrath" of God is not contrary to his love: it is an image
which becomes a moment of grace, because it permits us to perceive,
in a human way, the fact that the Lord is not resigned to accept our
refusal of him; even more so does it show that he knows how short-
lived are our days, how fragile our existence, how great our limita-

tions, our littleness. The long-suffering of the Lord is based on the fact that he "sees and understands that their death is miserable; and so he forgives them all the more" (Si 18:11). He does not judge or condemn but, thanks to his immense mercy, he awaits the proper occasion to change sin into a possibility of redemption, growth, and final grace.

We learn tolerance by watching how God treats his creatures and above all by contemplating that which Christ, the just one *par excellence*, did: the Face, the Heart, the Word of God. He "did not lift up his voice, or break the bruised reed, or quench the smoldering wick" (Is 42:2). He paid in person and invited his faithful to believe in love and to abide in love (cf. Jn 15). Christ did not hold back the difficulties which those who would place themselves on his side would experience: "You will be hated by all on account of my name: yet not a hair on your head will be lost. By your patience you will gain your souls" (Lk 21:17-19). Patience and tolerance are not required only sporadically or in moments of trial, but every day, because the believer is called to deny himself and "to take up his cross each day" (Lk 9:23).

Looking at the life and teaching of Christ, Paul did not hesitate to invite Christians to face tribulations with courage, to hope against all human hope, to make of the harshness of daily life a motive for growing in patience, because "affliction produces endurance, and endurance, proven character, and proven character, hope" (Rm 5:5).

WEEDS AND MERCY

Jesus tells this parable: "The Kingdom of Heaven has been compared to a man who sowed good seed in his field. While everyone was sleeping, his enemy came and sowed weeds among the wheat and went off, so when the shoots sprouted and bore fruit the weeds appeared then, too. The householder's servants came to him and said, 'Master, didn't you sow good seed in your field? Then where did the weeds come from?' He said to them, 'An enemy did this.' So the slaves said to him, 'Do you want us to gather them up, then?' But he said, 'No. You might uproot the wheat at the same time you're gathering the weeds. Let them both grow together until the harvest, and at the harvest time I'll tell the harvesters, "First gather the weeds and tie them in bundles to be burned, but gather the wheat into my barn"'" (Mt 13:24-30).

This parable enjoys the privilege of having been interpreted in an official manner by Jesus himself, in Matthew 13:36-43. The parable in itself, however, is offered to all without distinction, while the interpretation is reserved to his disciples alone who "after he left the crowds [and] went into the house. . . came to him and said, 'Explain the parable of the weeds in the field to us.'"

All the possible problems linked to evil in the world receive light from this parable:

— there is an adversary, an enemy who, profiting from the dark, goes about sowing evil precisely there where a good and conscientious person has sowed good works;

— good and evil, believer and unbeliever, virtue and vice have coexisted in the world from the very beginning and they will be common heirs of it to the end of time;

— the weeds (evil) are immediately obvious and seem to prevail over the wheat (good); the zealous will be tempted to intervene in a radical way, eliminating as much as possible that which could be an obstacle to the progress of good;

— the human being, however, must not take upon himself the right to judge (he can condemn a fact or a situation, but never a person); judgment is reserved to the Lord who, at the end of time, will rise up as a just judge;

— the present time must be characterized by waiting, patience, and tolerance;

— the disciples have to be aware of the fact that theirs is a sensitive mission which will be all the more fruitful the more it is freed of the temptation to be fanatic, self-righteous, and too demanding, and the more that they imitate the Lord who believes in the goodness of creation and waits for man to be aware of Him who came into the world, not to condemn but to save.

The world, which came forth from the hands of God, says the first pages of Genesis — was good. Humanity in its beginning was "very good." Immediately, however, the adversary sowed evil, which every man has experienced, ratifying with his own iniquitous acts that original sin. The world at the end of time will also be good. There will be a new creation, when Christ will hand over to the Father all of creation vivified by the Spirit. Alpha and Omega, beginning and end, are in the hands of God who entrusts the intermediate time, the time of mercy, to man.

Following Luke, the evangelist of mercy, in chapter six, in the discourse on the plain (the greater part of the people were not able to climb the mountain, and so Christ descends to meet the crowd where he found them), one immediately notes the radical quality of the choice of Jesus and what must characterize the "children of the Kingdom." It is expressed in the first Beatitude: "Blessed are you poor; the reign of God is yours" (Lk 6:20). And this law of poverty is concretized in a love extended to all, including one's enemies: "Love your enemies, do good to those who hate you, bless those who curse you. . ." (Lk 6:27). Why? The response is implicit for the poor person who feels pardoned, overwhelmed by grace, and already now an heir of the Kingdom.

Love requires respect for the other, for his time to understand and to grow. Love — as St. Paul says in the thirteenth chapter of his first letter to the Corinthians — believes all, hopes all, forgives all. Love does not judge. "Do not judge that you be not judged" (Lk 6:37). All are called to give, to forgive, and not to exchange evil for evil but to conquer evil with good, to eliminate misery from the earth, to live in that evangelical poverty which consists in despoiling oneself of all that is superfluous, so that every living being might have space in himself for others, for God first of all.

And to give God first place is the same as giving first place to the poor from the moment that Christ identified himself with the least, the smallest, the poorest of the poor. Only on this condition can a person be saved.

VI

Tolerance and Its Challenges: Truth and Religion

DOES TRUTH MAKE ONE INTOLERANT?

Truth — like mystery, attractive and fascinating — is not something enchanting and abstract but a reality which is "incarnated" with different aspects in diverse cultures and persons. Truth is one with the beauty, goodness, unity and harmony of creation, as St. Thomas Aquinas says (*"unum, verum, bonum et pulchrum convertuntur"*). Truth, as the shining forth of mystery, cannot make one intolerant, because it stirs up in us a sense of fascination and awe. Dogmatism, instead, can make one intolerant: those who think that they possess the fulness of truth falsify the mystery and automatically become intolerant, blinded by pride. Instead those who seek the truth are enriched by the knowledge that every person receives it from the very light of God himself.[1] Christ said that the truth will make us free.

---

[1] "The Old Testament attests that God is the source of all truth. His word is truth. His law is truth. . . Since God is 'true,' the members of his people are called to live in the truth.

"In Jesus Christ, the whole of God's truth has been made manifest. 'Full of grace and truth,' he came as 'the light of the world.' He is the Truth. 'Whoever believes in me may not remain in darkness.' The disciple of Jesus continues in his word so as to 'know the truth [that] will make you free' and that sanctifies. To follow Jesus is to 'live in the Spirit of truth,' whom the Father sends in his name and who leads 'into all the truth.' To his disciples Jesus teaches the unconditional love of truth" (*Catechism of the Catholic Church*, No. 2465-2466).

The moral law, too, has its origin in God and always finds its source in him. "At the same time, by virtue of natural reason, which derives from divine wisdom, it is a properly human law. Indeed. . . the natural law is 'nothing other than the light of understanding infused in us by God, whereby we understand what must be done and what must be avoided. God gave this light and this law to man at creation' (St. Thomas Aquinas, *In Duo Praecepta Caritatis*. . ., II, No. 1129). The rightful autonomy of the practical reason means that man possesses in himself his own law, received from the

Among other things, it will surely make us free from the presumption of having a monopoly on orthodoxy. It will free us from the prejudices that impede us from learning from every person, above all from the least and the poorest; it will free us from the fanaticism which leads us to persecute other human beings whom we consider to be less important to us than a principle or an abstract mental category.

One can never insist enough on saying that self-appointed "possessors of the truth" are blind. They no longer know how to seek and are dangerous to the faithful who feel weak, who tend to grab on to those who seem sure of themselves. Only the community of "disciples," who "learn" together, are on the way toward liberating truth. This idea was expressed by the First Vatican Council.[2] The popes have always used all the means at their disposal to keep themselves informed concerning all that the people of God believe, to search for the truth; the teaching Church is a co-learner with the Church being taught.[3] Infallibilism, the unwillingness to listen to others and learn from them, inevitably leads to error.

THE RECIPROCITY OF CULTURE AND RELIGION

There is a reciprocity between the specific culture of a country and the religion practiced in it: religious intolerance is grafted on to a determined culture; and a proud and self-sufficient culture pro-

---

Creator. Nevertheless, the autonomy of reason cannot mean that reason itself creates values and moral norms. Were this autonomy to imply a denial of the participation of the practical reason in the wisdom of the divine Creator and Lawgiver, or were it to suggest a freedom which creates moral norms, on the basis of historical contingencies or the diversity of societies and cultures, this sort of alleged autonomy would contradict the Church's teaching on the truth about man. It would be the death of true freedom." John Paul II, *Veritatis Splendor*, No. 41.

[2] Cf. Denzinger-Hunerman, *Enchiridion Symbolorum*, Herder, 1991[37]. *Pastor aeternus*, 28.7.1870, c. IV.

[3] This was the affirmation which permitted the approval of the dogma of infallibility, because this paragraph was intended not as a simple historical reference, but as a norm.

motes a type of intolerant religiosity. A classic example comes from the 1600's, in the Thirty Years' War which involved Germany, France, Switzerland and the Low Countries (Belgium, the Netherlands, and Luxembourg) in an unjust alliance between religion and politics. Everyone knows the motto: *"Cuius regio eius et religio"* ("He who controls the area controls the religion") which obliged the subjects to follow the religion of their sovereign. In those times, there was a real reciprocity of contamination between the interests of the monarchs who "used" religion and the religious leaders who took advantage of the political moment to enjoy a certain prestige and dominion over the consciences of the faithful.

One cannot speak in the abstract about the intolerance of religions, because it is always the *Sitz in Leben*, the culture, which favors fanaticism. On the other hand, and this is the painful side of our discourse, if religion were pure it would have the strength to cure the social ill of using the name of God for motives of power and prestige. A weak, superficial religion, bent on dogmatism and not on the fascinating and awesome mystery of God, leads to fanaticism and intolerance. In times past, men of the Church let themselves be instruments of the government and in part they themselves made use of the government for utilitarian ends. That happened mostly in the Protestant world, but the Catholic Church didn't do anything either to distance itself from the use of religion on the part of the powerful.[4]

As far as the Catholic Church, in particular, is concerned, a tendency present in many areas more or less covertly set forth this principle: Catholics where they were in the majority sought to have Catholicism made the religion of the State, while they invoked the principle of tolerance where they were in a minority.

Not a few people take for granted that a religion, simply because it considers itself to be the custodian of the truth, must necessarily be intolerant. A systematic study of religions dispersed throughout the world demonstrate the contrary if they are well lived. Here are some examples:

---

[4] Cf. K. Rahner, *Grace in Freedom*, New York, 1969, p. 238.

(1) Taoism has a strong bent towards tolerance and nonviolence. The sacred and the mysterious have given rise among
the faithful to that type of nonviolence which has great
therapeutic value on the personal and communitarian level.
The central idea which rules the moral life of the Taoist is
this: strength is to be found in weakness.[5]

(2) Islam lends itself to nonviolent and tolerant discourse. In
the Koran there are some passages which leave the problem
of violence open, but the central message is clearly nonviolent: "Men, we have created you from a male and a female
and divided you into nations and tribes that you might get to
know one another" (49:13). As a religion, Islam promotes
complete submission to God — in thought, word, deed,
belief and work — in view of complete peace for oneself
and for others. Again the Koran states: "Those who repent
and serve Allah and praise Him; those who fast and those
who kneel and prostrate themselves before Him; those who
enjoin justice, forbid evil and observe the commandments
of Allah, shall be richly rewarded" (2:112). The Koran
condemns those who threaten peace: "When a man turns his
back on peace, he lives on the earth doing evil and destroy-
ing life on earth. Allah does not love those who do evil"
(2:205). The Prophet does not hesitate then to affirm: "Your
God is one, you descend from Adam and Adam was created
from the dust: in matters of justice, an Arab is not superior
to a non-Arab, nor a white man to a black."[6]

As far as the so-called contemporary "Islamic fanaticism" is concerned, it has to do with a form of integralism
caused in great part by the provocations of the Western
world which the Muslims hold to be atheistic, only in

---

[5] Cf. A. Waley, *Three Ways of Thought in Ancient China*, London, 1939. H. Welch, *The Parting of the Way: Lao Tzu and the Taoist Movement*, London, 1958. Soo Chee, *Die Kunst des T'ai Chi Ch'uan. Der taistiche Weg*, Munich, 1986.

[6] Cf. R. Habibur-Chowdbury, *Islam e pace* in *Mosaico di pace*, June 10, 1991, p. 19.

search of money, and intent on rendering ever poorer the Third World. Besides, as far as the past is concerned, the Church, which ought to have been consistent with the message of peace of Christ its founder, instead provoked the Muslims by shutting them out, holding them in disdain and going to war with them: the crusades are the most striking examples. In the Islamic world we find the Egyptian sect of the "Muslim Brotherhood" which expresses its own identity by means of violence and in other countries there are fringe groups of fanatics. But one must not overlook the nonviolent currents in Islam. Apart from some violent fundamentalist leaders and their followers, the majority of the common people live in harmony with everyone.[7]

(3) As far as Buddhism is concerned, we must remember that we are dealing with a religion and not a philosophy.

The Buddhist has a very strong sense of mystery, because of which one must never speak of God in order not to risk trivializing or profaning the mystery simply by mentioning God's name.

In this religion there are no dogmas because the Mystery cannot be defined and cataloged by the human mind. The "enlightened" (*Botsatwa*) think of nirvana not as an emptiness but as the presence of life and joy, for which they have created a great missionary movement in an attempt to unite all human beings in the fulness of the communication of life. Buddhism, in its highest expression (*Mahajana*) has produced countless monks and men of prayer who have at

---

[7] Cf. C.M. Martini, *I nodi culturali del dialogo in una società di immigrazione con particolare riferimento ai gruppi di culture diverse da quella occidentale,* in *Solidarietà per le nuove migrazioni* by the 3rd International Congress of the Pontifical Council for the Pastoral Care of Migrants and Itinerant People, Vatican City, Sept. 30 - Oct. 5, 1991, pp. 185-197.
  To put the discourse into practice, it would be useful to study the thought of the Muslim president of Kossovo, Ibrahim Rugova in V. Salvoldi and L. Gjergji, *Resistenza nonviolenta nella ex Jugoslavia. Dal Kossovo la testimonianza dei protagonisti,* Emi, Bologna, 1993. Cf. also V. Salvoldi, *Islam, un popolo in preghiera,* Bologna, 1990.

heart peace between all the living. One can understand,
studying this religion, how great a fascination a relationship
with God freed from every form of dogmatism and of the
presumption of being able to say everything about Him who
by essence is ineffable and inexpressible can exercise on
Westerners. This religion is essentially nonviolent and
tolerant: it invites the faithful not to take themselves too
seriously but to develop a healthy sense of humor, laughing
at their own limits and powers, mere nothing in comparison
with the Mystery, and with the fulness of life and joy which
is the Absolute.[8]

(4) To understand Hinduism we can take Gandhi as a point of
departure. He discovered nonviolence in the Gospels, in the
Beatitudes, then found in the history of Hinduism many
analogies with the principal message of the Christian
religion. He centered his thought on the mystery of the new
man and on God who has compassion on human limitations,
is merciful toward men and pardons them.

All this is the source of a conciliatory, nonviolent,
peaceful and tolerant life, because it is respectful of every
person.

"It is unthinkable today to tackle the argument of
tolerance without having reference to the thought and
actions of Mohandas Karamchand Gandhi, known throughout the world as Mahatma, the 'great soul' (...) *Ahisma*
(non-violence) teaches us to maintain towards the religious
beliefs of another the same respect which we have for our
own, an admission which will be very simple for those who
seek the truth and follow the law of love. If we were to be
given the whole vision of truth — Gandhi says — we would
no longer be mere seekers, but we would be one with God,

---

[8] Cf. H. De Lubac, *Le rencontre du Bouddisme et de l'occident*, Paris, 1952. E. Lonze, *Der Buddhismus: Woher und Entwicklung*, Stuttgart, 1986[8]. H. Demoulin, *Begegnung mit dem Buddhismus*, Freibourg, 1978. H. Von Glasenapp, *Die Weisheit del Buddha*, Baden-Baden, 1946. H. Küng, *Christentum und weltreligionen: Hinfuhrung zum Dialog mit Islam, Hinduismus und Buddhismus*, Munich-Zurich, 1984.

for God is truth. But since we are still intent on seeking, let us pursue our search aware of our own imperfections. 'Nonviolence' and 'truth' are two words so closely linked that they can almost be interchangeable. *Ahisma* and truth — Gandhi writes — are so much one that it is practically impossible to separate them. They are two sides of the same coin, or better yet, of a smooth metallic disk, not yet engraved. Who can say which is the right side and which is the obverse? In spite of this, *ahisma* is the means and truth is the end. . . Truth resides in the heart of every man and it is there that it must be sought. No one, however, has the right to force others to act according to his way of seeing the truth."[9]

Both Hinduism and Christianity, in their purest expressions, nourished the thought of Gandhi and of several persons who, to this day, find in these two religions the strength to believe and the will to struggle for a world that is just, nonviolent and tolerant.

(5) Christianity could be the religion of tolerance by name were its faithful to live fully the mystery of the baptism of Christ in the Jordan. There the voice came: "You are my beloved son," a clear reference to the "Nonviolent" or "Suffering Servant" passages from the prophet Isaiah. Jesus on that occasion formally undertook to represent the new humanity which honors God by means of a choice for nonviolence.

If we Christians were aware of having been baptized in the name of Jesus, we would have to make our own his choice of being nonviolent, extremely respectful of the dignity of every person, and hence champions of nonviolence and tolerance.[10]

---

[9] Johanbegloo Ramin, *Gandhi e la lotta per la nonviolenza*, in *Il corriere dell'Unesco* 8-9 (1992), pp. 18-19.

[10] The first Christians, in fact, understood well what following the "Nonviolent Servant" might mean and so, for four centuries, they categorically refused violence, the fabrication of arms (they were even forbidden to design arms), and military service.

The Mennonites, the Quakers and the Waldensians have
placed a great deal of importance on this vision of nonviolence and tolerance, forgotten by the majority of Catholics
but kept alive by a prophet here and there, among whom St.
Francis of Assisi emerges as a symbol.[11]

A GLANCE AT CHRIST

Jesus made a great contribution to the theme of peace and
tolerance, teaching respect for all religions. His relationship with the
Samaritans is significant: whereas his fellow countrymen judged
them heretics, impure, schismatics, Jesus spoke with them, came up
with a parable which has a Samaritan as its protagonist and symbol
of the "saved"; he revealed to the Samaritan woman that the Father
wants to be adored not in a temple or on a mountain, but "in spirit and
in truth."
    One notes that as in Judea so in Samaria it was forbidden to
speak with a woman like the Samaritan woman, cast aside by four
men. Jesus totally rejects the moral and religious judgment of his
time and restores dignity to this heretical and excommunicated
woman, makes of her an "apostle," in opposition to all the prejudices
which held his fellow countrymen captive.
    Jesus knew neither frontier nor barrier: he had great respect for
everyone, because love exalts differences making of them common
riches. In the grandiose final vision of chapter five in the Gospel of
St. Matthew, Jesus makes a criterion of salvation: to have met the
Lord in the stranger, in the poor, in the least of one's brethren, in the

---

[11] Catholics today, if they wish, have at their disposition a theology which, reevaluating
the baptism of Christ and freeing itself from a false conception that the Father needed
the sacrifice of his Son to reconcile humanity, has the possibility of bringing together
other religions in the search for the truth, the good, tolerance and peace.
    With these principles, which are at the core of the Christian message and which are
present also in other religions, we have the possibility of comparing one "theology with
another" to see what we have in common and to find incentive for creating a new
humanity.

sinner, in the enemy become a friend. This passage paints Christ as the teacher of tolerance; he, the nonviolent person *par excellence*, presents the ideal of disarming the evil of the world with good, of converting hatred into love, of transforming vengeance through an offering of pardon, not once but seventy times seven times (always).

In his dealing with the Syro-Phoenician woman, the Gospel text lends itself to two teachings. The stranger asks a miracle of Christ and the Master responds, "It is not good to take the children's bread and throw it to the dogs." But faced with her reply, "Lord, even the dogs beneath the table eat the children's crumbs," Christ worked the miracle, after first praising the faith of the woman.

A first interpretation: Christ, being God, is also fully human and, as such, lets himself be taught by life, by events, by the persons whom he meets. In this case, he is grateful to this stranger and salutes her with admiration: "Woman, great is your faith!"

Another possible explanation: Jesus wanted to get this response, provoking an act of faith, capable of performing the miracle (elsewhere he said, "Your faith has saved you").

Respect for every human being is fundamental to the Christian religion, because every person, other than having value in himself, recalls the mysterious presence of the Lord from the moment in which "God became man, that man might become God." Here the pinnacle of the mystery is reached, understood not as an obscure reality, but as the fulness of light, which initially obliges one to worship in silence, in adoration, and then to immerse oneself in the reality for the purpose of working to build peace together with all persons of good will.[12]

---

[12] "Peace among peoples will not be possible if religions do not assume their specific role as bearers of peace." This is the central idea proposed by Hans Küng in Chicago in 1993 and almost unanimously accepted by the 6000 participants belonging to various religions. Every religion has the duty to dialog, to respect every human being, to make a precise stand for nonviolence. There will be peace on earth if religions themselves live in peace with one another in mutual respect.

VII

From Tolerance to Solidarity

"WE ARE ALL TRULY RESPONSIBLE FOR ALL"[1]

"No man is an island." We are not alone and, as believers in God, we must be jointly responsible for one another. There is in each of us an aspiration to unity even if in our daily choices we often live in isolation and do wrong. Thirty some years ago, the Second Vatican Council already brought this to our attention: "There is on the one hand a lively feeling of unity and of compelling solidarity, of mutual dependence, and on the other a lamentable cleavage of bitterly opposing camps. We have not yet seen the last of bitter political, social, and economic hostility, and racial and ideological antagonism, nor are we free of the specter of a war of total destruction."[2]

"The tragedy of groups and even of peoples forced into exile is recognized today as a permanent attack on the fundamental human rights of millions of persons. The situation of refugees, which strains the limits of human suffering, becomes an inescapable appeal to the conscience of all"[3] and forces us to reflect on the principles of solidarity and subsidiarity, in light of the passage from tolerance to

---

[1] *Sollicitudo rei socialis*, 38.

[2] *Gaudium et spes*, 4:4. Analyzing this passage, the Pontifical Council for the Pastoral Care of Migrants and Itinerant Peoples states: "The unsolved problem of refugees is a painful confirmation of this" (Cf. *I rifugiati, una sfida alla solidarietà*, Vatican City, 1992, p. 14).

[3] A document of the Pontifical Council, *op. cit.*, p. 23.

fraternity and for the sake of becoming aware that "we are all truly responsible for all."[4]

In the past, there was a lot of discussion to establish whether the basis for solidarity ought to be sought in the common descent of the human race from a single couple: monogenism. The true believer goes beyond the problem of monogenism and polygenism, since he bases the unity of every human being on monotheism. And we are authentic monotheists to the extent to which we live in solidarity, conforming ourselves to Christ, the Monotheist *par excellence*. He is the Prophet who breaks down all barriers. He is the High Priest, the bridge between heaven and earth. He is the King who unites believers in the one God and Lord, thus becoming himself our peace.

He who loves only his own people and not the other "tribes," the other groups, is not a monotheist, because he makes an idol of his ethnicity, excluding from his love the men and women for whom the Son of God gave his life.

Universal solidarity implies love even for one's enemy, because Christ, the only perfect being, the perfect Monotheist, prayed for his enemies and died for their salvation.

Solidarity lived in the name of Christ transcends the concept of tolerance, or better, gives it a new orientation and stimulus to surpass itself in light of a universal brotherhood. One could say that tolerance

---

[4] "Respect for the human person proceeds by way of respect for the principle that 'everyone should look upon his neighbor (without any exception) as "another self," above all bearing in mind his life and the means necessary for living it with dignity' (*Gaudium et spes*, 27:1). No legislation could by itself do away with the fears, prejudices, and attitudes of pride and selfishness which obstruct the establishment of truly fraternal societies. Such behavior will cease only through the charity that finds in every man a 'neighbor,' a brother.

"The duty of making oneself a neighbor to others and actively serving them becomes even more urgent when it involves the disadvantaged, in whatever area this may be. 'As you did it to one of the least of these my brethren, you did it to me' (Mt 25:40).

"This same duty extends to those who think or act differently from us. The teaching of Christ goes so far as to require the forgiveness of offenses. He extends the commandment of love, which is that of the New Law, to all enemies (cf. Mt 5:43-44). Liberation in the spirit of the Gospel is incompatible with hatred of one's enemy as a person, but not with hatred of the evil that he does as an enemy." *Catechism of the Catholic Church*, No. 1931-1933.

expresses all of its strength and is subsequently ennobled if seen in the context of a solidarity of salvation.

Naturally we know that there also exists a solidarity in evil,[5] but whoever chooses to be a monotheist and to live under the logic of the baptism of Christ, declares himself to be in solid communion with the good, with all the living, redeemed in the water, the Spirit and the blood (cf. Mt 3:11; 1 Jn 5:6).

THE PRINCIPLES OF SOLIDARITY AND SUBSIDIARITY

At the purely social and philosophical level — without necessarily having recourse to religion — the principle of solidarity can be understood as a reciprocal bond between human beings who are co-responsible for the good one of the other. The basis of such a principle is what we have said concerning the concept of monotheism and about the person as relation. We could say in a succinct way: "Each one of us is co-responsible for the good of every human being."[6]

---

[5] Saint Paul helps us to understand this "mystery of iniquity." "As through one man sin entered the world, and through sin, death, and in this way death spread to all men because they all sinned. . ." (Rm 5:12). The sentence shows an abrupt change to a second grammatical construction inconsistent with the first part. It is not completed because St. Paul, in his attempt to create a parallel between the first Adam, from whom death came into the world, and the second Adam, Christ, from whom life issues forth, realizes that he cannot place on the same plane Adam and Christ, because we receive much more from our solidarity with the Savior than from our solidarity with the sin of the first man. "So then, just as one man's offense resulted in condemnation for all, so too one man's obedience resulted in pardon and life for all. For just as many were made sinners as a result of one man's disobedience, so too through one man's obedience many will be made righteous. . . Where sin increased, grace increased even more" (Rm 5:18-20).

[6] The liberal culture, in years past, kept the concept of "solidarity" hostage, seeing in it an attempt at an unwarranted interference of the Catholic world into an economic process which ought to be managed autonomously, without having recourse to principles of an ethical or moral order.

Marxist culture likewise held this concept hostage, fearing that the Catholic world might propose a universal charity and a reward in the other life, contrary to the requirements of a radical change of society by means of a revolution against dominating unjust structures.

Whoever lives the principle of solidarity responsibly also honors that of subsidiarity, according to which it is illicit to give to individuals more than they can handle by themselves and it is unjust to expect a superior authority to do that which can be adequately handled by an inferior. This principle has the scope of favoring the participation of everyone in the realization of the common good, and of avoiding having a central organism impede groups and single individuals from fulfilling themselves through responsible and personal effort.[7]

If someone imposes himself on others and pretends to lead everyone from on high, he rejects that solidarity to which Christ alludes, affirming: "There is only one teacher, and the rest of you are learners."

Respect for the principle of solidarity leads to the principle of subsidiarity which requires the personalization of every relationship and the creation of elbow room so that all human beings can advance

---

Our society can, as a matter of fact, even having understood that solidarity is not a concept of which Christians have a monopoly and while also sensing all the urgency for such a virtue for the survival of the human race, still not live in solidarity. Today the tensions caused by the juxtaposition of classes do not exist, but we rather find the emergence of corporations, made up of groups of persons bound together by common interests: the individual members seek to overcome isolation and to satisfy the same needs, frequently finding themselves thrown together again in ways which are purely legal and pragmatic.

This situation is to be found clearly among the young, but it also touches the adults and the elderly, often intent on promoting the interests of their own group, not caring that they do so at the expense of others. One's own ego, the need to survive and to save oneself, emerges irrepressibly. Vaccinated against the evil of the world, inured to the catastrophic news of persons who continue to die of hunger or are killed by those belonging to opposing factions, challenged by the question of whether we do not feel co-responsible for the heap of iniquity which grips the human race, they respond: "Am I my brother's keeper?" And, unknowingly, by replying in this fashion, they declare themselves to be "Cain."

To how many is the common good of real personal concern? Who feels morally responsible when he or she defrauds the State, doesn't pay taxes, squanders what could be of common utility? How many work positively for the advent of a society which does not favor the North at the expense of the South of the world and places the premises for various people's coexistence, that they structure themselves after a great family, in which the good of one is a condition for the happiness of the other?

[7] This principle is resolutely expressed in the encyclical *Quadragesimo anno* and is the second pillar after that of solidarity in the social doctrine of Paul VI.

and multiply their talents, putting them at the disposition of the common good in a healthy reciprocity.

That goes for the family and for small groups, as well as for the State which should intervene only when the group is incapable of fruitfully carrying out its mission. Even the United Nations will be helpful if it promotes the autonomy of the single States and if these will live respecting the principles which we are analyzing. The identical discourse can be made for the Church, which should avoid presenting itself as a suffocating central organization which takes everything on itself, controls everything and gives directives to every part of the world, to the detriment of what the local and synodal authorities can decide for themselves.

An admirable example of subsidiarity is to be found in the election of the apostle Matthias as a substitute for Judas. The whole community is present and prays. Peter does not decide on his own: he prefers to draw a candidate by lot rather than to impose his will (cf. Ac 1:21-26).

To reformulate the principle of subsidiarity in a positive way, let us keep to this point: I, in solidarity with everyone else, do what I can to fulfill myself, my family, my group and all human beings reached by me, and I have recourse to superior authority only in cases of inadequacy or incompetence regarding important questions. In other words, I place my neighbor in the condition of giving his very best, so that all persons can feel themselves to be creative and satisfied in the search for the common good.

It is appropriate to continually look for ways to put this principle into practice, because there can always be in us the temptation to lord it over others or to resign ourselves to being served by others. In the family, the parents must educate their children not to have recourse to them when they can obtain by their own efforts a determined result. And so, for example, if two brothers are fighting, it is good that they learn by themselves how to make up and reestablish peace: the parents will be prepared to intervene only when it is absolutely necessary.

Also in social-political questions, citizens must not consider the State as an organism that continually intervenes to provide for the lack of initiative at the local and individual level. On the contrary, citizens must be educated to take pride in contributing to the general well-being of their own country and to establish funds to help poor countries or those impoverished by us.[8]

The Church, finally, which has well-formulated the principle of subsidiarity, must see to it that the individual faithful are able to exercise their own role fully, living that baptism which has made them "prophets, priests and kings," not dependent on the clergy. It follows that the Church, while it lives collegiality with all the bishops, should rule itself through permanent synodal structures both on the diocesan as well as the universal levels.

TOWARD A WORLD COMMUNITY

In the last twenty years, the proposal for planetary social justice has come up insistently.[9] One hopes for the advent of an era in which an authentic world community can be created in which the dignity of each one and the fundamental rights of all are recognized and in which every nation understands that it cannot think of its own welfare without interesting itself in the welfare of all nations.[10]

However, while we speak of a world authority, with power to bring order to the various nations, respecting the principles of solidarity and subsidiarity, we are witnesses to the phenomenon of nationalistic claims and ethnic tensions which often break out in

---

[8] A federal structure of the individual States of a United Europe is indispensable for promoting both subsidiarity and solidarity. Germany is a nation which is governed on the basis of federal principles: under the *länder* (the individual regions having a great deal of autonomy) the individual citizen enjoys an enormously stimulating situation. The central government does not intervene to develop an activity which can be handled by the *länder*. German federalism guarantees that the *länders* which are wealthier must contribute each year to help those which are more disadvantaged: fundamental is the redistribution of goods, and not only of those which are superfluous.

[9] Cf. G. and P. Mische, *Toward a Human World Order: Beyond the National Security Straitjacket*, New York, 1977.

[10] See the encyclical *Pacem in terris*, 68.

conflicts and wars. There are, in fact, contradictions in the development of history: new needs arise, bearers of a life-giving breath, while at the same time antagonistic forces, forces of death, explode on the scene. Thus movements are born which seek to suffocate the aspirations for good which are only in the planning stage.

The new, however, moves ahead in spite of the opposition. After the Second World War, with the organization of the United Nations, an effort was made to elaborate and promulgate a code of international law which would protect the fundamental rights of individuals and groups. Nevertheless, the United Nations still does not have the power to impose its will, nor does it have a legally authorized and authoritative representative. The time has not yet arrived to courageously propose such a world authority because up till now the narrow concept of the sovereignty of the Nation State still holds sway.

What we need is an "internal politics" which embraces all the world such that, in matters of fundamental rights, no person, no ethnic or religious group, no culture or subculture will feel themselves to be foreigners, "outsiders" in the world community. Humanity in its complexity must assume the duty of social justice for all people, for all groups, and for all individuals, in a way that no one can be considered simply an object. Everyone together must be subjects even with all their legitimate diversity.

If we have some faith in liberty and want to be faithful to the plan of God, the burden which we undertake in rejecting the idea of a super state, with the absolute power to impose its own ideology and dictates on all will never be excessive. If we succeed in seeing and in providing that a world-wide unification, and consequently a world authority, be put into place today, we must act in such a way that it becomes a reality by virtue of free consent, with all the essential guarantees and with all the space necessary for the spirit of liberty and of co-responsibility. If unification is not achieved according to these modalities, there will be the risk that such a unification be imposed by a superpower organized according to an ideology hostile to freedom.

The last few popes have clearly taught that it is necessary that a supreme world authority be created, especially in view of the promotion of peace and the care of the environment, on the basis of a concept of global social justice and in the context of the risks and opportunities for developing a unified global economy.

In his message to the General Assembly of the United Nations (Oct. 4, 1965), Paul VI expressed this conviction with great passion: "Your vocation is to make brothers not only of some, but of all peoples. A difficult undertaking? Without a doubt. But this is your task, your most noble task. Who does not see the need to achieve, progressively, the installation of a world authority, capable of acting effectively on the juridical and political planes?"[11]

But no sooner do we come up with efficacious structures than we drag our heels for fear of the "beast that comes up from the abyss" (Rv 11:7), for fear of universal tyranny. The remedy is not to be found in the renunciation of the idea and of the reality of some kind of world authority, but rather in putting into act everywhere, at every level and in every camp, federated structures based on subsidiarity. If such a principle is to become a reality in the mind, heart and will of all peoples, we will tranquilly entrust to this future world authority all the power which it will need to accomplish its great task of promoting peace and justice in respect for the fundamental rights of every person, without prejudice towards any of the functions which compete in the diverse cultural, economical and political communities.

While we nourish the dream of the coming of a world authority, it is good to sustain the movement initiated at Taizé, the council of young people which gets together every year in great numbers, in various nations, to pray, to examine what brings people together, and to establish the basis for a more just, ecumenical society, committed to work for peace. We would hope that such initiatives might be multiplied.

---

[11] *Insegnamenti di Paolo VI*, III, Vatican City, 1965, p. 519.

The Ethical Foundation for Solidarity

Solidarity corresponds to God's way of being: it is his own face seeking the human creature. In Christ, God makes himself completely one with every man and woman. He becomes in Christ, the Son of man, "one of us." He bound himself to the fate of every human being, to the point of saying: "Whatever you have done to the least of my brothers, that you have done unto me."

The continual reference to God in search of an ethical foundation for our action isn't done to convince one that solidarity is a uniquely religious and prevalently Christian value. Every religious and moral discussion is based on exquisitely human values because the God of revelation is the same God of creation: he manifests himself through analogous values among all peoples, since he is the Creator also of those who do not know Christ.

Dietrich Bonhoeffer expressed very well this concept, whose central idea we summarize here: Insofar as I am a Christian I must act as if I were always in the presence of God and at the same time I must feel thoroughly responsible for my actions as if God did not exist.[12]

This attitude can help me to be aware of my duties towards persons whom I meet, as if I were the last hope of the poor who knock at my door. For the simple fact of being a human creature, the destiny of humanity must be close to my heart: "I am human and let nothing that is human be alien to me" (Terence). However, before being for others, I must also be with others. I do not have as a purpose my fulfillment in helping those who are in need, but I accept to be as all the others, and I place myself on the level of the poor with whom I share the joy of being called "blessed."

The ethical category of responsibility obliges me not to bury the talents I have received, but to multiply them for the advantage of all.

---

[12] The phrase "as if God did not exist" refers above all to the image of a stopgap God, or of a distant, transcendent Being, wrapped in the smoke of incense. Christ wants to be sought in the poor and wills that each of us become bread for him, break his chains, clothe his nakedness, welcome him as a pilgrim, a refugee, one in search of work, and so forth.

The place in which my responsibility towards God, myself, others, and the cosmos is revealed is in my conscience where, in a unique and irrepeatable way the call is heard from God who expects a response not cut out of a mold but modeled on who I am. It is the call to discover with joy the sublime nature of my vocation, to be one reality with Christ, to bear fruit in love for the life of the world (cf. *Optatam totius,* 16), and to devote myself to bettering the historical cultural context in which I live with this basic attitude: while I await everything from God, while I pray because I know that salvation is exclusively his gift, I do all as if everything depended on me, "as if he did not exist."

TO GRADUALLY BECOME "HUMAN BEINGS"

To be a man is to become a human being through a process which obliges us every day to renew and to broaden our horizons. The Bible says: "The fool changes like the moon," but it also affirms: "It belongs to the wise man to be able to change." To which the intuition of John Henry Cardinal Newman makes echo: "To live is to change, and to achieve perfection means to have changed often."

In the evolutionary process, while we tend toward the ideal of being "perfect as the heavenly Father is perfect," we learn to be brothers through the observance of certain norms, dictated by common sense, as well as by the demands of the common good.

1. "The first (and most important) thing is to avoid doing evil to anyone." It would be ideal to be able to approach others as Christ did, "who went about doing good." When this is not possible, even because we often meet people who don't let you love them and who seem to be expert in changing good into evil, it becomes indispensable to do all that is possible so that our actions do not have a negative impact on others.

2. "Man is neither angel nor beast," Pascal says (*Pensées,* No. 358); "the misfortune is that he who would act the angel acts the beast." In other words: to expect too much of a person who only has one talent is to make him crazy.

Hence, it is fundamental to show ourselves to be tolerant and not to demand of an individual that which he cannot give. If his single talent is doubled, he will go into paradise with two talents.

3. It is necessary "to love justice," to use an expression taken from the Prophets. All have the obligation to go to the root of things, that is to say to try to be sure that power is exercised with justice, that wealth is honestly earned and used for the common good, that certain political and economical choices are for the common good and do not favor only one part of the world.

4. Besides the command to "love justice" and "to walk humbly with your God," the Prophet adds that the worship asked for by the Lord is to know how to love everyone with tenderness. To reach that point, it helps to train ourselves to approach persons, seeing in them seeds of truth, goodness and beauty.

5. For those who have faith, a big help in nourishing the virtue of solidarity is given by the thought that, since everyone has the same Father, "every man is our brother." And one can wash the feet of a brother or sister, as Christ did at the Last Supper. We can let a brother or sister wash our feet. We, who are tempted to the sin of taking the leading role, prefer to "wash the feet" of those in need. Perhaps it is more advantageous, every once in awhile, to let our feet be washed, that is to say, to let other persons shine and fulfill themselves, enjoying the room which will permit them to feel appreciated in doing a little good.

ROOM FOR VOLUNTARY SERVICE

To bind persons together, in an attempt to create a civilization not only of tolerance but also of integration and love, voluntary service has shown itself to be particularly important: e.g., the year which, in Italy or abroad, girls give to the common good in civil service at the end of their studies, or which boys who are conscientious objectors or who do not enroll in the army for whatever reason give who place themselves at the disposition of the community. Before getting into a discourse on the role which voluntary service ought to play and before asking if the presence of young volunteers makes a society responsible or serves as an excuse for some to unload on others jobs which ought to be done by all, it might be good to present some images: a young girl kneeling before an elderly woman, listening; another who is hand in hand with a blind eighty-year old; a young person who assists a man till he dies, whose illness lengthens into years.

It would be beautiful to be able to go into detail, but perhaps this brief flash will suffice to illustrate the slice which voluntary service and those who assume it will take with the passage of time: a discreet presence among little children, with those who have work-related problems, who suffer, with the needy, the sick, the elderly who are seeking to make sense out of life and death.

Speaking to the youth in Turin in 1988, Pope John Paul II stated: "I might even say that a young person of your age who does not give, in one form or other, some length of time to the service of others, cannot call himself Christian, such and so many are the demands which originate from the brothers and sisters around us." Voluntary service is not a monopoly of Christianity; on the contrary, without taking anything from Christian volunteers, in many countries of the "Third World" you can meet persons who, though not believing in God, are in love with humanity and who work gratuitously without being able to believe that ultimately there will be a Supreme Being ready to repay them for their sacrifices.

FROM SOLIDARITY TO UNIVERSAL BROTHERHOOD

At the beginning of 1971, Pope Paul VI addressed a message to the world which remains a kind of general policy statement for the social commitment of the Christian in the world. Speaking of peace, he said that "it represents *per se* the moral progress of humanity, decisively oriented towards unity. Unity and peace, when liberty unites them, are sisters."[13] The world is tired of war, absurdly considered as a necessary means for solving controversies. Human beings feel themselves to be bound by a closely-woven net of relationships based on culture, economy, sports and tourism: "A fundamental solidarity is forming in the world which favors peace."[14] Its foundation is a sense of justice, of an intangible human dignity, of the equality of all men and women, of human brotherhood.

Again, Paul VI writes: "This is our message for the year 1971. It echoes, like the voice which issues anew from civil conscience, the Declaration of the Rights of Man. All men are born free and equal in dignity and in rights; they are endowed with reason and knowledge and must conduct themselves as brothers one of the other. Up to this summit has ascended the doctrine of civilization. Let us not turn back. Let us not lose the treasure of this axiomatic conquest. Rather let us with logic and courage give application to this formula, the goal of human progress: every man is my brother."[15]

Tolerance, solidarity, peace, universal brotherhood.

Was Paul VI dreaming when he uttered this message?

To this question an oriental proverb responds: "Many times, thinking of a flower, I have seen it bloom."

---

[13] Paul VI, *Messagio per la giornata della pace*, Jan. 1, 1971 in *Acta Apostolicae Sedis* 68 (1971), p. 8.

[14] *Ibid.*, p. 7.

[15] *Ibid.*, p. 8.

VIII

Dialog for a Culture of Peace

THE THERAPEUTIC VALUE OF DIALOG

Health (physical, psychic and moral) is a relational concept. I am a healthy person to the extent that I have a constructive relationship with my self, with "you," and with "us." Speaking of "personalism" and of the thought of Buber and Levinas we partially anticipated what the best therapists have been saying: the very best expression of relationality is dialog which, when well used, creates relationships which are healthy and healing.

The first thing to be mentioned is that dialog, before being put into words, is founded on the senses: eyes which welcome into the self a person, handshakes which are exchanged sealing an alliance. The body sends out signals which create an interpersonal rapport. Dialog begins with listening, is strengthened through sympathy, and is made concrete in verbal responses.

To be fruitful dialog must abandon prejudice and make use of nonviolence, in virtue of which even the opposition is not perceived as an "enemy," but as a "you," who seeks and communicates values. Nonviolence is the "superpower" which heals every relationship thanks to its power to build and rebuild ties between persons.

The general well-being of a family depends a lot on that dialog which facilitates relationships, because if in the home the family members believe in nonviolence, if together they reciprocally place their trust in one another, they easily overcome little disagreements and various tensions, and they even find occasions for establishing an ever closer alliance. The same thing can be said of the local community, and the even larger family which is the entire world.

Dialog serves to placate souls, to enrich individuals thanks to the contribution brought by diverse persons, to bring about intellectual and moral growth. All of these things reflect a truly religious dimension: dialog, understood as an existential relationality, is found in am eminent way within the Trinity. The divine "I," "You," "We" are the foundation and building blocks of our interpersonal relationships, not permitting the believer to live in insignificant relationships or to fall into moralism since God makes himself the guarantor of noble and creative relationships.

A Dialog Among Cultures

To make an absolute of one's own culture is a sign that one belongs to an idolatrous society. Instead, to consider the whole human family and all cultures taken together with respect, willed by God as a harmonious concert of thousands and thousands of voices, will bring us to look on the "different" and the "Third World" as potential resources and as a challenge to our ethnocentric and idolatrous tendencies.

Before thinking of the cultural contribution of the members of the Third World in our midst, it should be mentioned that in Italy as in Germany,[1] their physical presence is an important one, not only because our demographic growth is below zero, but also because such a presence makes concrete and historical our relationship with other cultures. This rapport takes the shape of enrichment and healthy challenge, which frees us from racial prejudices, from closing in on our own cultural world, and it enlarges our horizons enormously.

Our experience in diverse nations, above all in the Third World can be significant: what we have received morally and psychologically is much more than what we have been able to give. For us, now,

---

[1] The Germans have experienced the value, even from an economic point of view, of the movement to their nation of Italian immigrants whom they badly needed and who are still not yet fully integrated. Certainly, initial prejudices and racial tensions now in large part overcome, were not absent initially.

to make a preferential choice in favor of the poor is neither a burden nor simple obedience to a moral imperative, but a privilege. How much fruitfulness, even in our literature, is born precisely from the wealth of the stimuli received by persons belonging to different cultures. As a Chinese proverb states: "It is worth more to see a thing once than to study a thousand books about it."

A few examples suffice and we ask pardon for the inevitable generalizations. The joy of being welcomed by the penetrating gaze of the Pakistanis, the pleasant glances of the Mongols, the peaceful and pacifying look of the Brazilians (though the carnival of Rio de Janeiro is celebrated only during one month of the year, with the Brazilians there is always a carnival, and the warmth is imparted by their faces more than by their costumes).

In many African tribes, before any exchange of a business or educational nature takes place, there is always an exchange of smiles, greetings and the question, "Does peace reign in your heart, home and village?"

In the Indian subcontinent, one breathes in the values proposed by Gandhi. We meet persons who make themselves poor in order to share the common situation of the country and not to humiliate the simple people with an irritating attitude of superiority. They are persons who radiate — probably without knowing it — the message of the Sermon on the Mount, the light of the Beatitudes.

The simple observation of a dance permits one to capture the typical values of a people: the mysticism of the dance of the dervishes in Turkey; the impulse towards the transcendent in certain dances which mimic the poetic flights of Pindar in some countries of Northern Europe; the sense of mystical immanence in some African dances in which the dancers stamp their feet and face the ground where the spirits of their ancestors repose.

African liturgical dances are an expression of the profound religious communication of the members of a tribe who present themselves before God, moving every part of their body, praying with their body, speaking with their smiles. In this way they put into practice the truth of their conviction: "Even if we are poor we always have reason to be joyful and to dance before God."

To celebrate feasts together with the poor is a source of
enrichment and joy which those who have not had such an intercul-
tural experience can never imagine.

ECUMENICAL DIALOG

Awareness of our "catholicity" and attention to the "Son of
Man," representative of the new nonviolent humanity, obliges us to
address the theme of reconciliation with our separated brethren. We
need some fresh air and — as Paul VI says — to breathe with both
lungs. Beyond the metaphor, we must sincerely dialog as much with
the Orthodox as with the Protestants, brothers of East and West. We
Catholics need them, as much as they need us, to be reconciled in our
respective diversity and activities which favor the ecumenical movement.[2]

It's not so much a matter of going after clearer and more defined
concepts as it is a matter of overcoming a suffocating conceptualism
in order to create space in which we can adore the mystery of God in
common and communicate that mystery to humanity which struggles
so to believe.

In the dialog between Catholics and Anglicans, before beginning the discussion of a specific argument, each one is called to
witness how it lives a particular truth and how it is lived by their own
community. And so those values which are not lived are set apart and
the value of certain other lived truths is rediscovered. This type of

---

[2] The Catholic ecumenical movement, initiated by Yves Congar and other theologians,
was accepted by Pope John XXIII. One of the most famous expressions of this Pope
who began the Second Vatican Council was the following: "We must look for all that
unites and not that which divides us." He said to the observers from the various
separated Churches present at the Council that we Catholics had need of them. And
their mutual presence was a more eloquent testimony than many of the interventions of
the Council Fathers. Among the observers, the insistence with which the representative
of the Quakers, Douglas Steer, asked the heads of the groups of commissions that the
theme of nonviolence become a central argument for deepening the essence of
Christianity and for favoring ecumenical dialog was important.

experience is the source of great enrichment for all and ought to be taken as a model for dialog with all the other churches.

Catholics can be enormously advantaged in their dialog with their separated brethren. They can help us in the work of purification of so many less than edifying incrustations which accrued over the centuries. They can, besides, help us to live the baptism of Christ, already recalled as a privileged moment, favoring the birth of the new humanity, the dismantling of so many barriers, the proclamation of the will of God to create a people that is free, disposed to serve him and their brothers and sisters in a spirit of truth.

These ideas are carried forward in a wonderful way in the ecumenical movement of the Council of Churches that convoked huge assemblies in Seoul and in Basel, having for their theme: "Justice, peace and the care of creation." There the justice which heals, the nonviolence which is the sole force capable of promoting peace, the ecological question such as the peace and harmony of creation (indispensable conditions for saving the seed of man on earth and for conserving an environment in which it is still possible to live singing the praises of the Creator) were all addressed.[3]

Justice and peace are great themes which today are shared in ecumenical dialog. And to those who ask why Christianity must be

---

[3] In 1993, the Vatican published the "Directory for the Application of the Principles and Norms on Ecumenism."

In continuity with the conciliar document *Unitatis redintegratio*, it repeated the need for a just equilibrium between confessional identity and openness to others. The Directory is important, not only for its novelty, as much as for its method. It is the fruit of an inductive type of work for which the contributions coming from the base were taken into account. And the base (the theologians involved in ecumenical discourses) indicates the direction in which we must move if dialog is to be fruitful; it is necessary to know ourselves, not with a kind of abstract knowledge, as one might know a mathematical formula, but with that kind of knowledge which implies a will to profound relationships (one might say "know thy self"); to correct one another and, for us Catholics, to have the humility to let ourselves be corrected, after having asked pardon for such intransigence and so many past errors; to encourage one another, taking the best from the speaker ("to look for that which unites"); to transcend ourselves, to go beyond where we are, seeking not ourselves but Him who gives meaning to our search, Him who is always in search of us; and finally it is necessary to work together for a nonviolent world, for a culture of peace.

so interested in "shalom," the peace of the Risen One, it is easy to respond that, for a believer in Christ, this is not one of many elective or optional themes, but one of the fundamental arguments: Peace for us is not some*thing*, but Some*one*. It is our Lord, "Christ, our peace" (Eph 2:14). To dialog then with our separated brethren, or better yet to work along side them for peace, is already a joint work of evangelization which contributes to unifying and vivifying the human race.

DIALOG WITH OTHER RELIGIONS

Every relationship based exclusively on economic gratification, on giving with an eye to receiving, on interests of various kinds, becomes insignificant and ends in nothing. Instead, if we are purified of the tendency to be violent (in virtue of the baptism which identifies us with Christ) and aware that Christianity is the religion of a love which places itself at the service of others, ready to suffer rather than to cause suffering, we can with great fruit initiate a dialog with other religions, exchanging with them the most precious treasures of our creed. A relationship based exclusively on interests, more or less hidden, is less than human and certainly not "catholic," that is, not universal. A rapport based on gratuitousness, mutual respect, listening and dialog, brings us closer to God and betters our human relationships.

We must open ourselves to others not so much to teach as to learn. A dialog which looks principally to convert the other is not fruitful. If there be a conversion, this will be a pure gift; it will not depend on our eloquence but, besides the intervention of God, rather more on our joyous witness.

If all is gift, "all is grace." The best attitude for approaching another to dialog profitably is that based on gratitude to God who permits us to meet Him in brothers and sisters belonging to diverse religions. And the dialog will be all the more profitable the more the dialoguing person is convinced of his faith and wholly rooted in his own religion. We have nothing, in fact, ever to gain from a discourse with a person who is shallow, little convinced, non-practicing, inconsistent, and not well informed about the moral propositions of his religion.

If there is not a great sense of gratitude and of gratuitousness in the rapport, the beauty and significance of the relationship itself will be lacking. And where this beauty is not perceived, one can never appreciate the splendor of the truth or capture the mysticism of the Hindus, the search for the All in the emptiness of the Buddhist, the subtlety of the prayer of the Sufi (Muslim mystics), the strength to be found in the weakness of the Taoist, the unconditioned acceptance of God in the guest of those belonging to many traditional African religions.

TOWARDS A CULTURE OF PEACE

We have seen how inter-religious and ecumenical dialog is important in view of a tolerant culture, a culture of peace, understood as the fruitful reconciliation of persons who seek the harmony to live in a diversity of cultures and religions. In our day, writings continue to multiply of theologians and irenologists (students of peace) who speak very passionately of a tolerant culture and a civilization of peace which can only be realized if one has the courage to make a radical choice for nonviolence. See especially the book of James Douglass, *The Nonviolent Coming of God.*[4]

---

[4] Orbis Books, Maryknoll, NY, 1993. The author recounts how during his stay in prison, because of his demonstrations for nonviolence, he became friendly with the guards and then of the generals, extending a trusting hand to all in advance. A frank and respectful dialog has borne excellent fruit, because there is nothing more disarming than to hear one say: "I know that you, too, want peace."

Douglass explores the most interesting parallels between the situation at the time of Christ and our own. Jesus, who lived in anticipation of the destruction of Jerusalem on the part of the Romans and suffered on account of this prophetic vision of his, preached a radical change in order to avoid the worst ("If you do not change and become nonviolent, you will perish"), an irreparable tragedy. The choice, then as now, was between nonviolence and nonexistence.

But even while everyone is speaking of nonviolence, while the dream of a new era of peace is very much alive, even after the fall of the Berlin wall, the fires of war, vindication, racial tensions, ethnic conflicts and wars within and among peoples, continue to increase without measure.[5] This happens because in many societies pride in

---

The hermeneutical message used by the American theologian is important:
— What did he really say?
— What was his past experience?
— What was the situation of the apostle when he wrote his Gospel?
— In what situation are we living the Gospel today?
We can better understand the thought of Christ if we frame it in the evolution of the Old Testament, where one clearly sees how God prepared his people, making them pass from violence to the hope of salvation obtained by means of the willingness of the "Nonviolent Servant" to sacrifice himself rather than others. God is gradual in his approach to his people because he is the merciful, patient, tolerant one *par excellence*. In the midst of a violent people, God exercises an excellent pedagogy of nonviolence: see how he raises up prophets who fight against the arrogance of those who hold themselves to be just, perfect and justified in doing violence to the non-believers, those "not chosen."

In the vision and testimony of Mahatma Gandhi, Martin Luther King, Oscar Romero and other apostles of nonviolence, Douglass sees signs of the Second Coming — in a nonviolent way — of God. And he concludes with the idea that a different future for humanity depends on its different choices: not the logic of power, but the nonviolent one of the cross of Christ.

[5] August 1994. The United Nations put out a bulletin of war: an atlas of conflicts. It speaks of the separatist war of Abkhazia (along with our conscience, our memory of geography is also in crisis). It speaks of the civil war in Afghanistan, of the tensions in Albania over Kossovo, of the internal conflicts in Angola, of the wars in Armenia and Azerbaijan. We are still in the letter "A" and already we are filled with anguish.

We have to avoid saying things like: "There are 65 countries at war." To the listener this is just a number and, unfortunately, to the people, used to hearing such catastrophic news with thousands of deaths, numbers don't mean anything any more. We must make a detailed list of the countries at war, after having first said that behind each name there are enormous dramas of mothers who will never see their sons any more, of men who have killed so many persons, of young people who instead of believing in love, will always believe more in violence.

It might be psychologically useful to paint in black, on a map of the world, those countries at war: the horror of a planet which so much egoism and ferocious violence are reducing to a ruinous cemetery would immediately be apparent. It would be just as useful if, at least in special times during the liturgical year, the priest from the altar, before intoning the "Gloria" would have the courage to list the names of those countries at war, inviting the people to say: "Lord, have mercy!" every time the name of a country at war was mentioned:

ABKHAZIA (separatist war), AFGHANISTAN (civil war), ALBANIA (tension over Kosovo), ALGERIA (internal conflict), ANGOLA (war), ARMENIA (war), AZERBAIJAN (war), BASQUE PROVINCES (struggle for independence),

belonging to a noble race, a great culture, a strong, beautiful, intelligent, hard-working and productive people is still deeply rooted in the culture. Pride of caste or religion; the pretence of having a monopoly on truth are still very much alive.

What a squalor when churches are transformed into places in which banal, non-committal discourses are held, and acts to justify the status quo are condoned, in which sermons are made which do not move the conscience, do not proclaim that the tree of peace is the tree of the cross!

So, without a prophetic spirit, can our Eucharists say of us that we are, as Turoldo affirmed, "Voices which implore justice, basins of tears, wine waiting to become blood"? Our celebrations cannot create the "prophet, priest and king" if the man is lacking, because either we are men of peace or we cannot be members of the new redeemed humanity.

BOSNIA (war), BRAZIL (death squads), BURMA (repression), BURUNDI (civil war), CAMBODIA (internal conflict), COLOMBIA (internal conflict), CONGO (internal conflict), CROATIA (Yugoslavian war), CUBA (embargo), CYPRUS (tension between the Greek and Turkish zones), DJIBOUTI (inter-ethnic conflict), EASTERN TIMOR (struggle for independence), EGYPT (internal conflict), EL SALVADOR (death squads, interruption of the peace process), EQUATORIAL GUINEA (repression), GEORGIA (war), GUATEMALA (repression, guerrilla war), HAITI (repression and embargo, now hopefully resolved), HONDURAS (repression), INDIA (internal conflict, tension with Pakistan), IRAN (repression and anti-Kurdish struggle), IRAQ (embargo), IRELAND (struggle for independence), ISRAEL (massacres and repression, peace process threatened), KENYA (internal conflict), KOSOVO (struggle for independence), KURDISTAN (repression and guerrilla war), LEBANON (war and Israeli occupation), LIBERIA (guerrilla war), LIBYA (embargo), MACEDONIA (tensions with Greece), MALAWI (bitter internal tensions), MOROCCO (tensions with Western Sahara), MEXICO (struggle of the Chiapas Indians, assassination attempts), MOLDAVIA (civil war), NIGERIA (military regime), NORTH KOREA (tension with the USA and South Korea), PAKISTAN (massacres and repression, renewal of the Intefada), PERU (repression, guerrilla war), PHILIPPINES (internal conflict), RWANDA (bloody civil war), SENEGAL (internal conflict), SERBIA and MONTENEGRO (Yugoslavian war, embargo), SIERRA LEONE (civil war), SOMALIA (internal conflict), SOUTH AFRICA (danger of internal conflicts reappearing), SOUTHERN OSSETIA (separatist war), SRI LANKA (struggle for Tamil independence), SUDAN (internal conflict, repression), TAJIKISTAN (civil war), TAMIL (struggle for independence), TOGO (internal conflict), TURKEY (repression, anti-Kurdish struggle), VENEZUELA (repression), WESTERN SAHARA (creeping guerrilla war), YEMEN (North-South conflict), ZAIRE (internal conflict).

That there be peace, it is indispensable to find a heart ready for conversion, for uprooting from itself the temptation to possess, to dominate the land, to subject other human beings.

Aggressivity and violence with respect to persons who surround us are love repressed: we would like to communicate and we are not able to do so. We would like to express our tenderness and instead we freeze up. We would like to embrace many people, and instead of giving them caresses, we give them blows, first in play, then out of habit, and finally as a vice. And love repressed explodes in malice, abuse of power, jealousy, envy and violence. The man is lacking! The community is lacking! Lacking, too, is that humanity for which Christ prayed during the Last Supper: "Father: that all might be one!" If the man of peace is not born, the human race will disappear from the earth because there are too many arsenals of death, too many mines strewn in every corner of the world, too many atomic bombs which could explode disintegrating all humanity.

St. Paul says that the birth of Christ made "humanity appear" on the face of the earth. All of our attempts against humanity sadly show that Christ was born, lived, died and rose in vain, even for many Christians. How many try to follow the Sermon on the Mount, the Beatitudes? Who practices turning the other cheek? Who — following the logic of St. Paul — considers his loss a gain? How many try to create relationships of reciprocal trust and tolerance?

In the Christian conception, at the basis of all tolerance there is the conviction that, behind those who have differing ideas, there is the same God, the Father of all; there is Christ, the common brother of all humanity; there is the Holy Spirit, who makes of us one body. Apart from his error, there is a human being whom we recognize and whom we cannot judge (cf. Rm 12:18ff.); apart from the provocation of the "enemy" who challenges us, there is the brother whom we must treat according to the requirements of truth, charity (cf. Eph 4:15), and humility, attitudes with which we reappraise ourselves and value others more.

We, who have more than once experienced the mercy of God, must be merciful towards others, pardoning, respecting, even loving all as God loves us, gratuitously. And it is precisely this capacity to respect everyone and everything, this complete tolerance, that is the presupposition for a culture of peace.

I, a man, humanity, must have respect for the goods of this earth which are not unlimited. I must use all sparingly, walk on tip toe so as not to disturb others, have recourse to clean and renewable energy sources, not consume or devastate what is indispensable for the good of the human race dispersed throughout the earth.

I, a human being, a creature, must treat other persons not as objects but as subjects who interact in a common, profitable dialog, open to love and to life.

I, a human being, king of all creation, do not have absolute "dominion" over other creatures or the goods of the earth, but only a capacity for vital relationships, similar to the power which the sun has over the planets, that is, an attraction in view of universal harmony.

I, a human being, a brother of Christ, the God who though rich made himself poor, if I want to be a Christian cannot have relationships of exploitation and oppression vis-à-vis the world and my fellow human beings, but must be poor, love's beggar, free of things, enamored of everything and everyone, like St. Francis of Assisi, poor for love, in love with creation, a living symbol of peace.

I, a human being, a child of God, must be a brother to every person and must discover God in all human beings and, in them and with them, sing "Glory to God in the highest," with the knowledge that the glory of the Most High is peace here on earth among the human beings whom He so loves.

PEACE IS BORN OF THE REQUEST FOR FORGIVENESS

In September of 1994, Pope John Paul II launched an impassioned appeal from Zagreb which should become the general policy statement of those who have intuitively sensed the value of tolerance and who want to become men of peace. In martyred ex-Yugoslavia, the Pope called for a new way of living together in the Balkans and insisted on the concept that peace is not a utopia. On the contrary, "it imposes itself as a prospect of historical realism."

In his homily, in fact, John Paul II explained: "For centuries the peoples of these regions have mutually accepted one another, developing a wealth of exchanges in the area of art, language, literature, popular culture. Is not the tradition of religious tolerance also a common heritage which throughout the interval of almost a thousand years has never been lacking even in the darkest periods? No, the phenomenon of nationalistic intolerance that is sweeping over this region cannot be attributed to religion!

"This is not only true for the Christians of various confessions whom God is calling today to make an extraordinary commitment to achieve full communion, but also for believers of other religions, especially the Muslims, who have built up a conspicuous presence in the Balkans, within the framework of respectful and civil coexistence."

For the Pope it is a matter of "a way of unity and peace which no one can avoid. This is demanded by reason, even before faith." Some have read in this passage of his homily the hope of a renewed united Yugoslavia, but that was disavowed by the same Pope when, in his farewell discourse at the airport, he underlined the fact that every people not only has the right to align itself with other peoples, but even to leave the federation and establish an independent State. He affirmed that each one of the republics of the former Yugoslavia has "a right to its own sovereignty, and cannot be denied international recognition."

But from the Pope also came a strong warning against nationalism and against the temptation to impose oneself, even for legitimate reasons, with violence. In his first discourse, at the moment in which he arrived in Croatia, he said: "Who does not remember Vukovar, Dubrovnik, Zadar and so many other Croatian cities and villages, smitten by the hurricane of war? Having come to an end in Croatia, the fighting unfortunately spread to neighboring Bosnia and Hercegovina. How much innocent blood has been shed! How many tears have lined the faces of mothers and children, old people and young ones!" Then he immediately added that "we need to promote a peace-loving culture, inspired by sentiments of tolerance and universal solidarity.

"This culture does not reject a healthy patriotism, but keeps it far from exaggerated nationalism and narrowness." Then, becoming concrete, he asked that the leaders of "this noble nation's public life may always follow a path of peace, comforted by the international community's support in order to solve the difficult and delicate problems which are still pending, such as those concerning the sovereignty of the entire national territory, the refugees' return and the rebuilding of all that has been devastated by the war."

For Christians the job is even more urgent because, as the Pope affirmed at the race-track, "Would it not be intolerable hypocrisy to repeat the 'Our Father' while harboring feelings of resentment and hatred, or even ideas of retaliation and revenge?" Then he added: "It is time for the Church in Zagreb and in the whole of Croatia to become promoters of mutual forgiveness and reconciliation. 'To ask forgiveness and to forgive'."

THE EDUCATION OF THE SENSES TO TOLERANCE

Having spoken of dialog to create a culture of peace, we feel it useful to conclude our tract on tolerance by pointing out the value of educating our bodies to dialog with the senses, in view of accepting other human beings. The "other" is encountered by us with a certain face which often sends an immediate message of acceptance or revulsion. There are some who, as soon as they see a person of another race from afar, for example, get upset. Others cannot endure certain body odors; still others get a bad impression from the harsh accents of a foreign tongue, or the taste of foods which are strange, or the manner of greeting, and so forth.

We have seen how such diversity can create problems which can be partially resolved by educating the senses to consider bodily contact with diverse persons as a richness: such an operation will be facilitated for those who think that every human being is a child of God, a person like himself.

It is necessary to educate ourselves to discover the beautiful in apparently upsetting situations: to see a baby born can be a traumatizing experience, but it can also seem like a miracle. St. Thomas says that a person perceives reality, coloring it with his own feelings. If one is beautiful inside, he discovers beauty in others; if he has the heart of a "brood of vipers," he will be tempted to see evil everywhere.

It is necessary to educate ourselves in an ethical and esthetic reading of the human body, of whatever body, understood as a stupendous microcosm.

And hence it is useful to discover the beauty of the five senses which permit us to capture the marvel of another.

Sight

Our eyes can take in others as an asset or a threat, while they can serve as an instrument for communicating the best of ourselves or for humiliating the other. In a context of religious esthetics, under the influence of the ancient Greeks, we must see the other as a stupendous microcosm which offers us immense intellectual and affective resources. In a Christian logic, the face of the other is the face of God himself. One's glance, however, must be educated because, according to the Bible, the eyes of the proud can humiliate and intimidate. Or, if they are tuned to the Lord, they can absorb his mercy which can then be poured out on every mortal being.

Hearing

The word of the one at our side must sound like music to our ears; the sound of the footsteps of a friendly person should make our hearts leap in our breast: "Hark! my lover — here he comes, springing across the mountains, leaping across the hills" (Sg 2:8). We must train ourselves to the use and hearing appropriate to the voice: "Do not raise your voice," our teachers and family members taught us. However, they also spurred us on to have the courage to speak up when something needed to be said, especially when all the hypocrites kept quiet. To educate one's hearing, to put oneself in tune with the most eloquent silence of all, God, is to educate oneself to the word, which is an echo of the eternal Word.

Smell

The Song of Songs eulogizes the perfume of the person loved. Perfume and name, in Hebrew, are synonymous. From the body of the beloved, the sacred author says, there emanates a perfume like incense: he comes up "from the desert. . . laden with myrrh, with frankincense, and with the perfume of every exotic dust" (Sg 3:6). Be educated regarding perfume: see how the beloved renders herself beautiful and perfumed to spend a pleasant evening, walking into the sunset, talking about herself, making a gift of gestures filled with grace and mystery.

Taste

When a mother lets herself go in outpourings of affection toward her little child, she says, "I could eat you." And she covers her child with kisses. There are those who say that the kiss is a harking back to the cannibalistic rites of old. And still the Song of Songs surprises us, right in the very first verse: "Let him kiss me with the kisses of his mouth." And it is significant that, at the Last Supper, other than experiencing the pleasure of eating together, Christ asked his Disciples to eat his flesh.

Touch

Shaking hands with others seals an understanding, communicates strength, says more than a thousand words. But the hand which caresses can also be used to strike. Here is where the obligation to teach a baby above all to use his body as a means for communicating love begins. It is necessary to teach people to free the love that is in each one of us. It is necessary to show that intolerance in an aggressive form could be avoided provided that the other is perceived "not as an enemy, but as a guest," not as competition, but as an angel who approaches us to show us new ways to make our existence more meaningful and beautiful.

— CONCLUSION —

The Pleasurable Aspect of Tolerance

The hard work in being tolerant is a particular aspect of the difficulty which each one of us experiences in trying to do good. Even if the good fascinates us, attracts us and turns out to be fun (the pleasurable aspect), to aspire to it is also always something difficult. It is not by chance that evil often seduces us because of its immediate ease.

It would be less than human to present tolerance as an effortless goal of the person who wants to dedicate himself to being virtuous. One has to overcome anguish, prejudice and fear in order to welcome another into one's own life. At the same time, it would be erroneous to present tolerance solely as hard work. There is a cheerful and pleasurable aspect to tolerance. Good generates joy.

The ethical path from tolerance to solidarity involves a passage from the category of duty to that of pleasure, the duty and the pleasure in doing good; from the duty to respect the right of a neighbor to be himself, to exist, to live with dignity according to his own culture and creed, to the pleasure of positively and joyously welcoming the other as a bearer of good.

To welcome the other becomes a source of spiritual pleasure which comes about by being close to the good which is known, chosen and put into practice. The system of ethics which evaluates the morality of actions in terms of their capacity to produce happiness (eudaemonism) affirms this: the practice of virtue generates happiness. Spiritual pleasure, then, is the result of the good which conforms us ever more to Christ. A person who has a purely sensible and utilitarian concept of good and pleasure will never appreciate and understand the joy of the spirit, a joy which involves the whole person but which has its roots in that aspect of ourselves which is modeled after the Holy Spirit, Love.

To do good, in other words, implies an esthetic joy; a relationship with many persons allows us to gather from all a fragment of truth and beauty which is hugely rewarding. Every human being comes into the world with his own message to communicate, each one is unique and irrepeatable. Dialoguing with and loving whomever we encounter, we gather enormous potential for being, for beauty and for love. Each encounter is new just as each day, each Spring, is new. Hence even prolonged relationships with the same person, are inexhaustible sources of novelty and freshness.

This esthetic level, however, is not enough. It is necessary to be able to gather together the diverse relationships of humanity as facets of the one face of God who calls and accepts in us every human being, thanks to the grace of the Spirit who leads us to make our own the choices of Christ. We can conform ourselves to his message to the extent that we identify ourselves with his person, reproducing in ourselves the same sentiments which he had, forcing ourselves to pass in the midst of suffering with the will to convert its limitations into grandeur. It is what St. Francis of Assisi suggests: "When they persecute you, insult you, and refuse to accept you, Brother Leo, write this down as well: this is perfect joy." It is necessary, in the way from tolerance to a solidarity based on brotherhood, to know how to follow in the footsteps of Christ, thus lessening the painful aspects of identification with the Crucified.

It is good to know the good and it is good to do the good. Kant said that there existed nothing more fascinating in the universe than the starry sky above us and our conscience deep within. The starry sky represents the harmony of the cosmos and the marvel of its laws; our conscience represents the joy of doing good, in conformity with the principle "to act in such a way that every personal deed could be elevated to a universal norm."

It is good to know and to act morally, always keeping in mind, however, that our existence is eminently conflictual. Hence our knowledge, while it lends itself to laud and thanksgiving, also weeps bitter tears over the lack of humanity and the cruelty of so many human choices.

This humanity, seed of the divine, is also stamped "by the insidiousness of the Evil One, who sows weeds." The weeds are not to be uprooted: God will burn them at the end of time. In the world there is more wheat than weeds. There is more good than bad. There is more tolerance than what appears in the news reports of the mass media.

There are people who spend their lives with the single ambition of alleviating the suffering of those in need, giving to all the gift of their smile — and the smile is precisely the most transparent image of tolerance. It is very important to be able to smile before certain daily realities, before those who persecute us, insult us, do not accept or love us. A smile costs very little, but it can fill a life and be a sign that one has passed from tolerance to solidarity, communion, and love. The general ideal of older generations which is proposed to modern civilization as a motto for tolerance can be summed up: in the search for truth unity is indispensable; in facing that which is doubtful or in dispute, there must be freedom; in every choice, in every human attitude, in every relationship with another love must reign. "*In necessariis unitas, in dubiis libertas, in omnibus charitas.*"

Bibliography

Aa.Vv., *Il rapporto Nord-Sud: popoli, etnie, nazioni nel Mediterraneo* (research and documentation under the direction of the *Centro Eirene* and of the *Cesvi*), Bergamo, 1993.

G.W. Allport, *The Nature of Prejudice*, Boston, 1954.

E. Balducci, *L'uomo planetario*, Fiesole, 1990.

M. Barbieri-Stefanelli, M. and B. Nicolini, *Zingari, Rom e Sinti*, Casale Monferrato, 1991.

B. Bellerate, *Pensiero prevenuto e ideologia in Orientamenti Pedagogici*, 38 (1991), pp. 327-336.

J. Blattner, *Toleranz als Strukturprinzip*, Freiburg, 1985.

G. Bocchi G. - M. Ceruti, *Solidarietà o barbarie. L'Europa delle diversità contro la pulizia etnica*, Milan, 1994.

D. Bonhoeffer, *Ethik*, Munich, 1966.

P.C. Bori (editor), *L'intolleranza: uguali e diversi nella storia*, Bologna, 1986.

M. Buber, *I and Thou*, Edinburgh, 1971.

M. Buber, *Two Types of Faith*, New York, 1951.

M. Buber, *Il principio dialogico*, Milan, 1990.

M. Buber, *Il problema dell'uomo*, Leumann, Turin, 1983.

M. Buber, *L'eclissi di Dio*, Milan, 1990.

S. Budner, *Intolerance of Ambiguity as a Personality Variable*, in *Personality*, 30 (1962), pp. 29-50.

F. Cardini, *Noi e l'Islam. Un incontro possibile?*, Bari, 1994.

E. Damoli - A. Lovati, *Carcere e società. Oltre la pena*, Casale Monferrato, 1994.

F. Dassetto - A. Bastenier, *Europa, nuova frontiera dell'Islam*, Rome, 1988.

J.W. Douglass, *The Nonviolent Coming of God*, New York, 1993.

W. Eichrodt, *Theology of the Old Testament*, 2 vols., London, 1961-1967.

M. Eliade, *Il mito dell'eterno ritorno*, Rome, 1982.

V. Frankl, *The Doctor of the Soul*, New York, 1965.

E. Fromm, *Psicanalisi e religione*, Milan, 1982.

A. Gesche, *L'homme*, Paris, 1993.

J.W. Hauer, *Toleranz und Intoleranz in den nichtchristlichen Religionen*, Stuttgart, 1961.

H.D. Johns, *Paura. Collera nel quotidiano*, Assisi, 1994.

F. Lenoir, *Il tempo della responsabilità*, Turin, 1994.

C. Levi Coen, *Martin Buber*, Florence, 1991.

E. Levinas, *Totalité et infini*, La Hoya, 1961.

E. Levinas, *Trancendance et intelligibilité*, Geneva, 1984.

I.M. Macioti - E. Pugliese, *Gli immigrati in Italia*, Rome, 1991.

G. Marcel, *La dignità umana*, Leumann, Turin, 1984.

G. Martina, *Tolleranza*, in *Dizionario storico religioso*, Rome, 1966.

A. Maslow, *The Farther Reaches of Human Nature*, New York, 1973.

A. Mastantuono, *Volontariato*, Casale Monferrato, 1994.

F. Molinan, *Tolleranza* in *Dizionario enciclopedico di teologia morale*, Rome, 1985.

J.H. Newman, *Apologia pro Vita Sua*, London, 1887.

K. Rahner, *Toleranz in der Kirche*, Freiburg, 1977.

P. Scilligo, *Gruppi e persone in conflitto: vie psicologiche alla solidarietà* in *Orientamenti Pedagogici*, 38 (1991), pp. 285-302.

P.A. Schlipp - M. Friedman, *The Philosophy of Martin Buber*, Illinois, 1967.

R. Schultz, *L'unità, speranza di vita*, Brescia, 1966.

A.D. Smith, *Le origini etniche nelle nazioni*, Bologna, 1992.

K.-R. Spillmann. *L'image de l'ennemi et l'escalade des conflits*, in *Revue Internationale des Sciences Sociales*, 127 (1991), Unesco.

G. Von Rad, *Teologia dell'Antico Testamento*, Brescia, 1975.